฿LOCKCHAIN
BASICS
INTRODUCTION
HANDBOOK

BLOCKCHAIN BASICS INTRODUCTION HANDBOOK

A Practical Non-Technical Guide for the Blockchain Beginner

MICHELLE SIMMS

with

ANDY EARLE

KEEP UP PUBLICATIONS

Published by Keep Up Publications
3150 Orleans St #28392
Bellingham, WA 98228
www.KeepUpPublications.com

Printed in the United States of America

First Edition: October 2022
Paperback ISBN 979-8-9868710-0-4

I will instruct you and teach in the way you should go;
I will counsel you with my eye upon you. - Psalm 32:8

About the Keep Up Publications Team

Want to understand what blockchain is without all the jargon?

You've come to the right place

Keep Up Publications is a project that is helping people understand how everything we do in the world will change due to the blockchain technology.

When the internet was introduced into the mainstream in the 1990's, no one could have imagined just how much it would change the world. We think blockchain technologies will be even bigger!

Started by a lifelong learner with a diverse background in life experiences, public and private education, and many different interests...Keep Up Publications is a team dedicated to empowering the individual to understand the blockchain from a beginner's perspective.

Our Philosophy is – Keep Learning, Keep Growing, and Keep Up!

Our blog is where, as an online community, we are mastering blockchain basics for the beginner using a step-by-step process presented in layman terms. Join us as we discover the power of the blockchain, and we explore how organizations and industries are reinventing themselves using this new and exciting blockchains technology.

Follow us on our journey as we publish our first book. Blockchain Basics Introduction Handbook: A Practical Non-technical Guide for the Blockchain Beginner is written in an entertaining way using stories, humor, and examples that everyone can relate to.

Most importantly the book breaks down all the technical complex jargon!

Thanks for stopping by and we look forward to sharing this amazing journey with you!

Cheers,
Keep Up Publications Team
www.KeepUpPublications.com

฿LOCKCHAIN
BASICS
INTRODUCTION
HANDBOOK

A Practical Non-technical Guide
for the Blockchain Beginner

MICHELLE SIMMS
KEEP UP PUBLICATIONS

CONTENTS

INTRODUCTION

The Curse of Knowledge

Why are new concepts so difficult to understand? When we want to learn about a new concept, our first instinct might be to seek out an expert. However, having expertise on a subject doesn't automatically make someone the best teacher. And yet, there is something compelling to beginners about engaging with experts on their craft.

There are dozens of platforms for experts to teach lay people about new concepts, subjects, or trades. If you want to learn how to train your dog, you can watch *Dog Whisperer*. If you want to learn all about cooking, you might try Bobby Flay's cookbook. And if you're not sure what you want to learn, MasterClass' online subscription service is packed with videos of experts giving lectures in their fields. But most people with a MasterClass subscription would agree that, while the videos can be entertaining, only a select few have real educational value.

Too often, when experts try to explain a subject to a learner, they fall into the trap called the Curse of Knowledge. The Curse refers to one's inability to know what someone else *doesn't* know. Experts might think they're delivering new information perfectly, but after an hour of speaking only in abstract terms full of industry-specific lingo, they can leave students more confused than when they started.

Experts spend so long looking at the big picture, they forget how confusing the details look to first-time viewers. When Cesar Millan from

Dog Whisperer tells his clients to "walk your dog like the leader," what is he asking them to do? When Bobby Flay writes, "add wine and stir until completely reduced," how would a beginner know what "reduced" wine looks like? Annie Leibovitz's MasterClass on photography tells viewers to "use natural light as a teacher," but even amateur photographers know the sun can't show them how a zoom lens works. Other experts in their fields may know exactly what these masters are trying to relay to their students, but the students are left with a twisted look of confusion on their faces.

The Curse can affect more than experts, too. Anyone who has already experienced a subject, and then tries to relay it to another person, can suffer from the Curse of Knowledge. The Curse has followed us since the beginning of time. Look no further than the medieval German series *Der Naturen Bloeme: The Flower of Nature*.[1] The book is full of animals that look completely unrealistic because the artists relied on descriptions from other people. A snail is shown with a wolf's head poking out of his shell. Another claims to be a hippopotamus, but the creature has the feet of a dog, the body of an armadillo, and the trunk of an elephant. It might seem silly for an artist to get it so wrong, but have you ever tried describing a hippopotamus to someone who's never heard of one? It's tougher than you think.

The Curse of Knowledge happens to all of us. Whether we're Stanford professors delivering lectures about spacetime or parents teaching our toddlers to read *Goodnight Moon*, we struggle to think about what our listeners don't know. Once we know something, we find it hard to imagine *not* knowing it. Our knowledge is considered a curse because when we try to relay it to others, we can't figure out where to start.

When the Curse of Knowledge leads people to assume their listeners know more about the foundation of a subject just because *they* know it, no one learns anything. It's like trying to line up books in an office without a bookshelf—all that knowledge falls flat. This is especially problematic in group sessions like seminars, business meetings, and

---

[1] https://publicdomainreview.org/collection/jacob-van-maerlant-der-naturen-bloeme

classrooms. When listeners are missing the foundational knowledge they need to understand, but no one speaks up for fear of looking stupid, everyone is worse off.

Let's say you and a group of friends sit down to play a card game. Your friend chooses *Go Fish*, but three of you have never played, so she explains the rules before she deals out the deck. She explains the winner is the one with the most "books" of cards. Aces are high, twos are low, and suits don't matter. Then she hands out seven cards to each player and throws the rest in the middle, swishing them around until they're a messy pile on the table. She tells your other friend to go first since he's sitting to the dealer's left. He sorts his hand, then asks you, "do you have any Kings?" but you haven't touched your deck yet. You're still trying to figure out what a "book" is.

If you don't speak up, you'll never know how to win. But if you do speak up, you risk being teased for not knowing—or at least intuiting—what a "book" is. Your friend didn't mean to put you in a bad position. She followed along with her instructions in her own head, but she filled in the gaps with her own knowledge. You don't have the benefit of her knowledge if she doesn't relay it to you. You've become another victim of the Curse, and so has your friend.

Not even teachers are immune from the Curse of Knowledge. Educators may have more training to help them avoid the Curse, but even the most thoughtful teachers slip up and skip over the basics. This is especially the case at higher levels of education. In fact, my worst experience with the Curse came from a professor on my first day of college.

I dropped out of school before finishing eighth grade. When I returned two decades later, I didn't have the same foundation of knowledge as my classmates. Still, I was dedicated to finishing my education. After sailing through my first few high school courses, a counselor recommended I sign up for a few community college classes at the same time. I didn't see the problem with doing both at once—I didn't know enough about education to recognize the problem with my plan.

I signed up for a college level English class without completing my high school English courses. I didn't know it at the time, but by the end of the first class, the Curse of Knowledge would threaten not only my ability to finish school, but my success any time I tried to learn about a new concept, skill, or process.

On the morning of my first day of community college, I felt out of place. I was only thirty-two years old, but as I watched the class fill with bright-eyed, bouncy eighteen-year-olds, I felt like a senior citizen. Not a single student carried a backpack; the girls used oversized purses and the boys had messenger bags. I shrank into my seat, kicking my JanSport under my chair. I buried my head in the textbook until the professor took his spot at the head of the class.

"Good morning, everyone!" he chirped, tossing his canvas bag on the desk. Even *he* looked younger than me.

"We're going to start out easy today," he said. "I want each of you to write me an essay. It can be about anything you want. I just want a basic understanding of where everyone is at. The subject doesn't matter, but don't forget the three main parts of an essay."

I froze in my seat.

"You have one hour," he said. "When you're finished, hand your paper to me and head out."

The classroom filled with noise from rustling papers and clicking pens. The professor looked up at the clock and nodded at us, signaling us to begin. I couldn't move. All around me, students put pen to paper like it was nothing. The professor pulled a book from his bag and started reading. The clock on the wall ticked louder. I tried to write something, *anything* on the page, but I couldn't think past the last part of the assignment.

Don't forget the three main parts of an essay.

I didn't know them.

My eyesight blurred with tears. I blinked rapidly to beat them back. I wasn't sure what to do. *Should I ask the professor? Maybe he forgot to explain,* I thought, but I quickly dismissed myself. *If he thought anyone wouldn't know, he would have explained it. He didn't think anyone could be that stupid.* I looked around the room to see if anyone else felt lost, but if they did, no one showed it. *Everyone else is writing. Everyone knows except me.* I didn't want anyone to catch on to me, so I spent the rest of the hour doodling on a piece of paper, trying not to cry.

One by one, the others packed their bags, handed their papers in, and walked out of the room. I kept on doodling until I was the last student in class. I sheepishly made my way up to the professor's desk. He looked up at me and almost smiled, but he saw my face and gave me a concerned look instead.

I set my doodles on the desk between us. I swallowed hard, but my throat felt too tight to speak up. If I tried to explain myself, I'd burst into tears right in front of him.

"I don't have anything for you," I said in a small voice, "and I'm sorry, I can't talk about it right now because it's taking everything I've got not to start crying."

His concern expression changed to one of confusion, but he didn't respond. I hung my head and made my way to the door. I'd never felt so ashamed. I wanted to turn the corner and never show my face in the building again. But before I could close the door behind me, the professor called out to me.

"Hey," he said, "be in my office tomorrow morning."

The next morning, the walk to his office felt like a walk of shame. His door was open, but I knocked anyway. He waved an arm toward the overstuffed armchair across from him. I took a seat and sank deep into the cushions.

"So, let's talk about yesterday," he said.

As we talked, I braced myself for him to scold me, or to kick me out of his class, or to tell me he'd never met a student so stupid in his life. I thought he might laugh at me when I told him why I'd handed in a page of poorly-drawn critters instead of an essay. Worst of all, I feared he would see my age, hear my story, and look at me with pity. Every time I finished talking and he opened his mouth to respond, I felt myself wincing, waiting for the moment when I'd leave for the last time...but it never came.

Instead, the professor told me he'd get me up to speed so I could keep up with the class. For the rest of the semester, I met with him twice a week: once for class and once for his office hours. He helped me build a foundation of knowledge I could use to keep up with his lessons. In one year, I earned my high school diploma and my transfer degree.

The professor didn't mean to isolate me on that first day. He simply didn't take into consideration that there might be someone in his class who didn't know the three parts of an essay. Like most experts, he didn't realize he'd fallen victim to the Curse of Knowledge. Sometimes, no matter how educated or experienced at teaching some experts are, they leave out the most important, foundational information to help their learners follow along. Since finishing my education. I'd experienced the Curse of Knowledge a handful of other times, but I could always work around it...until I began researching blockchains.

Blockchains are a new and exciting technology, which presents two issues: there is a limited amount of factual information available, and there is a lot of speculation about where the technology can lead us. It's impossible to figure out what is fact and what is fiction in our blockchain research if we don't have a strong foundational knowledge about what the blockchain is and how it works.

When we, the average readers, try to research blockchains, we only find resources that skip over the basic elements of explanation. Research papers, instructional videos, and even most "beginner" books about blockchains fall victim to the Curse of Knowledge. The materials build off of a foundation of technical lingo, abstract concepts, and dense explanations. As true beginners, we can't get past the first ten minutes of research without a gnarly headache and a knot in our stomach.

Since blockchain technology is still emerging, there are few true experts out there. There are even fewer who understand blockchains outside of the world of cryptocurrency, which is where the first blockchain saw its debut in 2009. The majority of the materials out there titled "Blockchain for Beginners" quickly enter into the world of cryptocurrency and never leave. Cryptocurrency is certainly part of blockchains' history and future, but it's only one of an infinite number of possibilities for blockchain application.

In simple terms, if we think about cryptocurrency as cars, blockchains are the road they travel on. Except in this analogy, the drivers don't need a license, the cars can't be used twice by the same driver, and the roads keep track of every trip ever taken on them.

You may start out overwhelmed, confused, or frustrated by the available research on blockchains. Even the Wikipedia page for "blockchain" starts out too complicated:

> *"A blockchain is a growing list of records, called* blocks, *that are securely linked together using cryptography. Each block contains a cryptographic hash of the previous block, a timestamp, and transaction data (generally represented as a Merkle tree, where data nodes are represented by leafs)."*

Now we know what a blockchain is, right?

Sure, that is if we also know the definitions for cryptography, cryptographic hash, timestamps, transaction data, Merkle trees, and leafs (different from "leaves"). If we don't, we have to spend the next half an hour looking them up, too. The cycle repeats with every new definition. Before we know it, we have a vocabulary list longer than the entire blockchain page on Wikipedia. Now we're tired, confused, and cranky, and the blockchain is to blame!

No one likes feeling confused or overwhelmed during their learning experience. The Curse of Knowledge is frustrating for new learners. We think if an expert is explaining, they must be doing it right. We want to scream, "Why am I not getting this? What's wrong with me?" We don't consider the issue might not be our fault, but the fault of the teacher. Then, we shut down our learning process altogether, because it's easier to give up than to admit we feel too far behind.

So, if we're not looking for an expert's explanation, where do we go to learn about the blockchain?

We learn together.

The best way for an educator to overcome the Curse of Knowledge is to write down what they learned as they learn it. When beginners make note of the important stops as they travel the trail of expertise, it becomes easier to follow the trail backwards. Then, it's even easier to lead others back down the trail, because the important landmarks are already laid out.

Before completing the beginner's guide in front of you now, I was a true beginner in blockchain technology. I read mountains of books on the subject. I watched videos and documentaries. I studied dissertations. As I studied, I took notes on what I wanted to know and the order in which I wanted to know it. I've collected everything I learned about blockchain technology and provided it here. I don't have a technical background, but I do have a passion for learning. When I began my research, I couldn't find a guide that answered questions on a true beginner's level, so I made it myself.

Since you're reading this book right now, I think it's safe to assume you, as a fellow beginner, recognize how influential the blockchain will become (or in some cases, how influential it is already.) Maybe your job is considering building a blockchain. Maybe you're looking to make a quick million. Maybe your group of friends won't stop talking about blockchains and you've decided if you can't beat 'em, you're going to join 'em. Whatever the reason for your interest in blockchain technology, you're already on the right track. You've made a choice to be proactive about your learning experience.

In this book, we are going to explore every corner of the blockchain from a beginner's point of view. By the time you're finished reading, you will have the strong foundation of knowledge you need to keep up with the blockchain as it emerges in everyday life.

CHAPTER 1

The Next Big Thing

Technology evolves at breakneck speeds. Many people assume they're advancing alongside technology and they're ready to embrace any changes new technology brings. Unfortunately, this assumption is as invalid now as it ever has been. The Next Big Thing in technology is already here, and most people know little to nothing about it.

It's not anyone's fault that we're unprepared for the Next Big Thing. It takes years for knowledge about a new tech innovation to trickle down from a small group of experts to the average, everyday user. Tech inventors are great at developing new ways for technology to benefit the everyday person, but they're not so great at teaching the everyday person how to use it.

Since most people aren't immediately able to grasp these Next Big Things right away, new technologies are often dismissed as a phase when the public first hears about them. When the iPhone was first announced in 2007, critics labeled it dead on arrival because of its fragile touch screen and weak battery. Decades earlier, people struggled to fathom how television sets would replace radios as household entertainment. And decades before then, a respected scientist in the late 1800s ranted about how harmful the printing press would be for society...in his first book. But today in 2022, printers, TVs, and iPhones impact most of our daily lives.

The Internet is one of the most influential technologies ever invented, but in its early years, more people were confused by it than excited about it. No one understood it well enough to imagine it would become essential in our lives. Although the Internet's official birthday is January 1, 1983, the average person then was still years away from booting up a home computer for emailing. In 1994, the hosts of the Today Show were still too busy debating what the "@" symbol meant to understand the Internet's potential.

"That little mark with the 'A' and then the ring around it," host Bryant Gumbel said, "I thought 'at' but Kate said she thought it was 'about.'"

"Or 'around,'" Katie Couric chimed in.

"What is the Internet, anyway?" Bryant asked. "What, do you write to it? Like mail?"

Bryant's head whipped back and forth between the two women on the couch with him. A man offscreen took his best shot at explaining the concept. The camera stayed on the couch while the three people on screen looked off in the distance with furrowed brows and crossed arms. They didn't realize that in 30 years, the clip of their innocent debate over an email symbol would become a famous example of how slowly the non-technical person catches on to disruptive technologies.

Most people in the early 90s, including myself, were in the same boat as Bryant and Katie. We didn't understand the Internet at all, much less how it would fundamentally change society. I didn't know how the Internet would change us, but every time it came up, electricity sparked through the conversation. I felt a tingling excitement when I heard people talk about it. I knew something big was coming.

Then, in the mid-90s, I watched as some of my coworkers in real estate were left behind by the new, fast-paced world of the Internet. They dismissed it as a "phase" and refused to learn about it. As the Internet popped into more conversations around my office's water cooler, I noticed my coworkers talking about it dismissively. They laughed, saying some newfangled technology would take the Internet's place in a few weeks, so they didn't need to pay attention. Then they walked back to their desks, scooped up their gigantic Multiple Listing Service books, and headed out the door to scope the new listings in their area.

I saw my coworkers rapidly lose out to competition as other real estate agents incorporated the Internet into their work. I worried that even after years of success as the top real estate company in the area, my office would slip into obscurity if we didn't take advantage of the Internet. If we didn't learn about this new disruptive technology and the changes it would bring, we'd be stuck in the past. I followed my gut and buried myself in researching the Internet.

Those who didn't keep up with the Internet lost their jobs. Some of the best realtors at our company disappeared from the office. The reams of paper usually covering office desks were replaced by computers. Instead of carrying around binders thicker than the platform shoes on their feet, realtors printed out single pages at a time from the Internet. The people who stuck around realized how much better our business ran, but I still felt horrible for the people who couldn't keep up.

Once our company cleared out realtors who didn't understand the Internet, business boomed. A new generation of people ready to embrace the Next Big Thing filled the empty seats. In this new digital age, those of us who remained had more time to spend on customer relationships because we didn't have to drive out to every new listing. We could conduct market research, schedule showings, and chat with buyers all from our desks. Fast forward to today's real estate practices, and a realtor can take a property from listing to closing without ever moving their feet. The time we saved on travel and logistics went right to our customers, and the tradeoff brought our office back to the top.

The Internet was one of the most influential and disruptive technologies the world has ever seen. It was also one of the last...until Decentralized Ledger Technology, otherwise known as "the blockchain" appeared. Have you heard of it?

Imagine a world where banking is intangible. No more paychecks, credit cards, or cash. You'll never touch a dirty dollar bill again. All of your money will still exist, but instead of storing it in one place, it will be stored in thousands of places at once. Sounds crazy, right? Well, buckle up, because it gets even crazier.

Not only will banking be intangible, but all personal information (voter IDs, driver's licenses, medical records) won't exist on paper anymore, either. It will all exist on the blockchain, where it's all accessible at any time, from anywhere...and it will never be at risk of being stolen, faked, or altered.

Some industries are in real danger from the blockchain. For example, the keychain industry is set to implode...because we won't need keys anymore. We won't have car keys, house keys, hotel keys, or even keys for bike locks. (Piano keys are still acceptable.) Surely this is ludicrous, though. When have humans ever not needed keys? The answer might just be a few years away.

People and companies who don't prepare to adopt blockchain will be left behind. In some industries, the blockchain is already here. If we're not educating ourselves on how it works and how we can use it, we'll be left in the dust, just like people who dismissed the Internet.

When I first heard about the blockchain, I felt a familiar electricity buzzing between conversations. I could sense blockchain would be the next big disruption to how our society functions. But when I sat down to research the new Next Big Thing, I didn't have as much luck as I did back in the 90s, even with the Internet to help me. I found myself drowning in information that was too dense, too technical, and too convoluted. Suddenly, I understood why so many people end up dismissing new technology instead of taking the steps to keep up.

The problem with the blockchain information available today is that it's written by experts who aren't breaking it down for beginners. Most guides to the blockchain skip over the foundation and dive right into the trickier implications of the technology. Even the majority of "beginner" guides on blockchain technology require a Master's degree, a PhD, or a decade of experience to understand. This technology could change everything about the way we live, but if people can't comprehend how it works and how to use it, it's going to create more problems than solutions.

I decided to take matters into my own hands, and that decision led to the book in front of you now. This book is a *real* introduction to the blockchain. A true beginner's guide. It begins with the most basic level of the blockchain and slowly builds a level of understanding from "I've heard of it" to "let me tell you all about it!" By the time you finish reading, you will understand what the blockchain is, how it works, and how it's going to change your life for the better.

There is no intelligence shaming in this book—no concept is too simple for a beginner, and no prior knowledge is too little. It's okay to think that blockchain miners sound like they're covered in soot, or that Merkle trees must grow nasty fruit, or that Proof-of-Stake is how vampire hunters confirm their kills. We'll break down each of those terms and more. And by the end of this guide, when the people in your office talk about blockchain, you'll be able to participate.

Not only will you understand the blockchain, you'll be ready to engage with blockchain technology directly. Later chapters predict future applications and explore how they can improve existing industries. You'll gain the knowledge to help your friends, families, and peers get on board too. When you hear your coworkers chat about cryptocurrency trends by the water cooler, you can grab a cup and jump in the conversation. It won't be long before you're able to invest in blockchain technology yourself, ending up with more money than Internet investors made during the dot com bubble.

But before we can channel 2000 Warren Buffett, we've got to channel 1994 Bryant Gumbel.

CHAPTER 2

Webvolution

No Next Big Thing in technology is born perfect. All new technologies go through cycles of improvement. They spawn as promising new solutions to specific problems, and eventually expand beyond their initial capabilities. Before the Internet gave western society cross-continental messaging capabilities, the communication methods were via telephone, telegram, and snail mail. To most people, this wasn't a problem, but when the threat of nuclear war peaked at the height of the Cold War, the U.S. military had real cause for concern.

Before comprehending what blockchain technology can do for the future, we must understand how the Internet has shaped the past. And to understand how the Internet evolved from its narrowly-used inception, we're going to dial our clocks all the way back to the 1960s.

The first iteration of Internet technology was designed to solve a single problem. In the event of nuclear fallout, could the military sound the alarm fast enough to protect its civilians? In the Cold War era, the answer was no. The U.S. military needed a faster, more reliable way to send a message across the country.[2]

---

[2] Bruttig, Spencer. "Here's How the Cold War Helped Create the Internet We Know and Love Today." wusa9.com, December 6, 2019. https://www.wusa9.com/article/news/nation-world/this-week-in-history-how-the-internet-was-created-during-the-cold-war/.

Some forms of near-instant communication existed in the 1960s, but they were too unreliable to transmit cross-country messages fast enough to protect people from a nuclear explosion. Computer and radio signals flowed through dedicated telephone lines across the country, but one severed connection could bring down the whole system. America's pre-Digital Age communication methods worked like a rickety bridge over a river of lava—no one who used it felt confident it would work as intended, and there was no guarantee it would hold for long.

The U.S. needed a way to communicate that could survive a disruption as big as a nuclear bomb. Researchers across the U.S. worked to find a fast solution, but they couldn't easily communicate their findings with each other, which only compounded the problem. And as the years ticked by and the Cold War tension escalated, people wondered if time was running out.

In 1969, the Department of Defense poured funding into an agency called the Advanced Research Projects Agency (ARPA) to solve the military's communication issues. ARPA designed a system called ARPAnet, a series of connected computers (or **nodes**) that used multiple telephone lines to send packages of information back and forth. For the first time, two computers had the ability to communicate instantly over a stable, digital foundation.

The first four nodes were connected from research facilities at the University of California Los Angeles, University of California Santa Barbara, Stanford University, and the University of Utah. These nodes could communicate instantly and relished the security of a decentralized network—if one node failed, the others maintained connections.

ARPAnet grew over the following decade, adding nodes from other institutions and government agencies. But before ARPAnet could grow into a stronger, more popular network, the U.S. government shut down ARPA and all its projects. As the threat of nuclear war dissipated, ARPAnet's funding was reallocated to other departments. The network dissolved in the late 1980s. However, researchers in California recognized ARPAnet's potential applications beyond the scope of the U.S. military.

ARPAnet blazed technological trails for what would eventually become the Internet. For example, when packets of information were passed through ARPAnet, users at each end used the @ symbol to address the data to a specific host.[3] This function laid the foundation for the first versions of email addresses. Researchers from connected laboratories and universities cobbled together some of ARPAnet's best features, like packet switching, decentralized computer networks, and even the @ symbol, to develop the earliest version of the Internet used in American homes.

When the Internet first appeared to the public, not many people believed it would be responsible for a new age in human history. The Internet's first iteration looked less like a limitless network of unimaginable applications and more like a dusty, half-empty library. It took decades for the Internet to expand enough for the average user to tangibly see its promise. Although the Internet's cycle of improvement is nowhere near complete, its ex pansion from Netscape to Netflix has revolutionized our world.

Web 1.0: The Read-Only Web

After ARPAnet's dissolvement, several of its researchers took the system's framework and expanded it for use outside of the military. This meant putting the technology in the hands of the public. By the early 1990s, the Internet had become a widely used (but underdeveloped) public resource.

In the Internet's early days, its research roots held strong. While the Internet itself belonged to no one, its physical infrastructure belonged to the National Science Foundation (NSF). This meant online content was still subject to the NSF's Acceptable Use Policy, which encouraged research-based content and discouraged any sort of advertising or commercial prospects.

---

[3] Techopedia. "What Is the Defense Advanced Research Projects Agency (DARPA)?" Techopedia.com. Techopedia, October 24, 2012. https://www.techopedia.com/definition/6727/defense-advanced-research-projects-agency-darpa.

In Web 1.0, the Internet worked like a library, and the websites within the Internet's network were the books. This version of the Internet was made up of static web pages. These websites looked like pages in a book, full of text and sometimes a visual aid or two. Text was black-on-white, graphics were grayscale, and users had just as much trouble staying awake in front of a computer as they did in front of an encyclopedia.

Experts call Web 1.0 the "read-only" web because there were no interactive elements available. There were no checkout forms, no user controls, and no place to "like" or share the information. Content hosted on each website looked the same for each user, no matter who visited.

Web 1.0 was considered a **Content Delivery Network** (CDN), which meant content creators could showcase information on a website and users could passively view it without providing feedback. Content came from a server's file system and was assigned to a spot on a website with frames and tables. However, in the early 90s, CDNs weren't easy to navigate, especially for users who didn't know how to program computers.

As everyday users dipped their toes into cyberspace for the first time, they felt understandably lost. They had a hard time comparing Web 1.0 innovations to technologies they were already familiar with. Sure, some parts resembled a research library, but books don't need keyboards, mice, or modems. And where do people return a website when they're done reading it? This confusion created a market for tools to help average users navigate the Internet.

Companies like Netscape and AOL made it a priority to design Internet navigation tools for the non-technical users. AOL modeled their homepage after a newspaper to give users a familiar structure. Netscape used embedded hyperlinks like trail markers to guide users from one web page to another. Tools like these allowed the Internet to become accessible for the average user. Some of the companies that jumped in early are still around today (Yahoo!, Google, Lycos), while others rose and fell with the dot-com bubble (AltaVista, Ask Jeeves).

Search engines and web guides made the Internet easy to use, even for people who didn't understand it. AOL, Hotmail, and other online clients gave people a chance to chat with each other instantly. Sites like MySpace gave non-technical users a place to build their own personal profile. People bought personal computers for the first time now that they could easily participate online. By the late 1990s, more than half of U.S. households had a personal computer connected to the Internet.

The Internet's increased accessibility brought droves of people online, which spawned many Internet-based businesses looking to cash in on a new market. The NSF's "Acceptable Use Policy" started as a strong guideline for new Internet presences to follow, but by the late 1990s, the policy was a plywood dam holding up against a flood of advertisements, paid services, and commerce sites. It couldn't hold for long, and in 1995 the dam finally broke. NSF handed the Internet over to private companies known as Internet Service Providers (ISPs).

The NSF's abdication from ruling the Internet ended the information era and ushered in a new reign. The earliest ISPs (CompuServe, America Online, Earthlink) dedicated massive amounts of time, money, and research into expanding Internet access. Since none of these companies had their own massive, cross-country infrastructure to provide Internet to their customers, they used existing phone lines. This meant no one in a home could use the phone and the Internet at the same time. This era is known as the Dial-Up era, and anyone online in the mid-90s through the mid-2000s remembers their modem hissing and clicking like an angry banshee while it connected to the Internet.

While an increasing number of Americans subscribed to the Internet, for-profit businesses developed tools for generating online income. Google launched AdWords and kicked off Internet monetization. Amazon appeared as one of the first entrepreneurial sites only weeks after the NSF's handoff. A new market for online investors opened for business, but before these venture capitalists could bring about the new e-world, their bubble of success popped.

One dot-com executive, Michael Wolff, reflected on the bubble afterwards in a 1999 cover story for *New York Magazine*.[4] He remembered why the true believers in the Internet's potential were so quick to bet their financial security on new online ventures.

"There is, at the elusive center of the e-experience, the fantasy that we might become free of economic laws," he wrote, "All it takes to make otherworldly riches is the will and desire."

The dot-com pop felt like a massive betrayal of trust to the average American. While big time investors pulled out their money in droves, smaller investors went broke; 100 million individual investors lost $5 trillion on the stock market. By the end of 2002, 70 percent of 401(k)s lost at least one-fifth of their values, and 45 percent lost even more.[5] People who began as the Internet's biggest supporters sold their computers to keep food on the table, and their dreams of a new economic future died alongside Netscape, CompuServe, and Pets.com.

Although the dot-com pop brought down Internet investments, Internet usage never declined. In fact, between the years of the pop—1999 and 2002—Internet traffic numbers soared to all-time highs. The years following the crash saw massive online improvements designed by the people most burned by their online investments. They were motivated to revolutionize the Internet with a new model for success—one where users could control the content.

Web 2.0: The Social Web

If Web 1.0 functioned as a bridge for safely transferring information, Web 2.0 marks the Internet's expansion into a two-way street used all

---

4   Schwartz, John. "Dot-Com Is Dot-Gone, and the Dream With It." The New York Times. The New York Times, November 25, 2001. https://www.nytimes.com/2001/11/25/style/dot-com-is-dot-gone-and-the-dream-with-it.html.

5   McCullough, Brian. "A Revealing Look at the Dot-Com Bubble of 2000 - And How It Shapes Our Lives Today." ideas.ted.com, December 4, 2018. https://ideas.ted.com/an-eye-opening-look-at-the-dot-com-bubble-of-2000-and-how-it-shapes-our-lives-today/.

over the world. There is no hard line between Web 1.0 and Web 2.0, but most experts agree the change came somewhere around the turn of the century, after the dot-com crash and before the first viral Tweet.

The shift from a "read-only" Internet to a "read-write" Internet marks the biggest change between Web 1.0 and Web 2.0, but even that distinction is a little fuzzy. AOL's chat rooms and some early versions of online bulletin boards are considered part of Web 1.0 even though they allowed users to interact on the sites. Experts consider these exceptions to the rule, because Web 2.0 allowed direct interactions with websites and returned user-generated data instantly.

Companies formed applications around a new "Web as Platform" concept, building directly on the Internet instead of on each desktop. For the first time, users didn't need to purchase additional software to make digital accounts and participate in online activities. This opened the doors for user-centered content like blogging, social networking, social media, video streaming, podcasting, and more. People could share their thoughts, feelings, and perspectives with others through a number of online platforms.

Many Internet applications transformed from CDNs to CMSs, or **Content Management Systems**, that gave users more freedom online. Even users with limited online expertise could add, modify, and remove content from a website. Static web pages were replaced with dynamic sites with ads, forms, and visuals that changed to best fit each user's Internet experience. Twitter feeds, Facebook home pages, and Yahoo! News headlines looked completely different depending on which users logged into the sites.

Web 2.0 was not only more customizable—it was also the beginning of the collaborative Internet we know today. Facebook users could "poke" each other to say hello. Users on Flickr could tag others in their photos. eBay users could provide feedback after making a purchase or selling an item. Likes, hashtags, shares, and other interactive user controls brought the web experience from singular to social.

As the Internet filled with user-generated content, providers realized they could make just as much money off of their customers as their products. Content creators with massive online followings started getting paid for producing videos and articles. Rating systems extended to real-world assets through services like TaskRabbit for freelance workers, Airbnb for homeowners, and Uber for ride sharing. These platforms depended on user-created content to keep them afloat, and the users were so excited to participate, they didn't think about how much value was behind their input.

The rise of smart devices like iPhones, Samsung Galaxies, and Google Pixels encouraged Internet-based services to include mobile applications. Cloud computing provided unlimited storage options, which allowed Internet businesses to move away from skyscrapers full of centralized servers. Users could create content at any time from anywhere. Companies could store the content remotely and host it on their platforms. The Internet became a place for people to commune, connect, and coexist. But there was a dark side to this social web.

While more users could create and publish content online, they lost ownership of it the moment they clicked the "Share" button. Corporations made millions and offered pennies to the people who made them rich. Middleman businesses appeared as trusted third parties for online transactions, but they collected a chunk of the profit and the user data in exchange. And these business models have only grown to be more efficient.

Personal data collecting business models have flooded the Internet. Companies publish their best online reviews to attract more customers. Shopping sites keep track of "recently viewed" items to tailor users' home pages to their shopping habits. One rainy afternoon someone might casually look up movies playing in theaters, only to be bombarded for the next week with ads for a new superhero action flick.

In the last gasp of Web 2.0, the more we use online resources, the more online resources use us. It's nearly impossible to shop, read, or explore online without creating a separate account for that website. Cookies keep track of our every online move and sell the records to the highest bidder. "Liking" Aunt Sally's Facebook picture of her morning bagel affects which ads Facebook shows. Web 2.0's original social connection has evolved into social commerce, and many users are ready to move on to the next phase: Web 3.0.

Web 3.0: The Semantic Web

The line between Web 2.0 and Web 3.0 is, like the previous evolution, a little murky. Some experts believe we're already in the midst of Web 3.0, but most agree we've barely scratched the surface. This iteration is known among experts as the "read-write-execute" web, or the Semantic Web. The hope is for automation programs to take the place of user-driven Internet activity. Here, data is not owned by anyone, but it is shared with services that display different views for the same information.

In the Semantic Web there are dynamic applications, interactive services, and automated processes that will take over the majority of what we do online today.[6] Machines won't simply take keywords from users and deliver matching results—they will comprehend the words we give, both in context and concept, and use them to bring back the best possible solution to our request.

Think about a trained dog who knows how to play fetch. His owner tosses a tennis ball and says, "Fetch!" and the dog grabs the ball and brings it back. He didn't grab the ball because he understands the word "fetch" means "retrieve and return this yellow tennis ball to my owner's hand." All the dog knows is the sound his owner makes when she says the word "fetch" means if he grabs the ball, brings it back, and drops it in his owner's hand, he will receive a treat (or at least a nice scratch on the head.) This is how Web 2.0 searches work.

---

[6] Verma, Pragati. "Evolution of Web." DEV Community. DEV Community, June 21, 2021. https://dev.to/pragativerma18/evolution-of-web-42eh.

Instead of using context and comprehension to follow orders, dogs are only capable of using context. The dog gathered all of his owner's input—she threw the ball, she made a sound with her mouth, she watched the ball bounce away—to figure out his next move. The dog is also already trained to follow this process when he receives the same inputs. He doesn't understand the situation any further than *I do trick, I get treat.*

Now, imagine the owner says, "Fetch me a pizza," and expects her dog to be successful. This genius-level dog sticks his nose in his owner's purse, grabs her wallet with his teeth, opens the front door, trots two streets down to Larry's Pies (he skips Gionni's because he knows his owner thinks their crust is too greasy), walks up to the counter, pokes the pizza on the menu he knows is his owner's favorite, offers cash from the wallet to the cashier, collects the change, waits for the pizza, and carries it back home. He makes sure to stick the wallet back in the purse before he delivers the receipt and the pizza to his owner's waiting hands.

That's Web 3.0.

The Semantic Web means machines will process information in a humanlike way through Artificial Intelligence and Machine Learning. Our smartwatches will read our heart rate and tell our coffee pots to start brewing as soon as we wake up. Our refrigerators will order new eggs the moment we take the last one out. Our cars will automatically start up fifteen minutes before we leave for work on a snowy morning. In Web 3.0, our devices don't simply know our patterns—they know us.

One of the biggest issues of Web 2.0 is that our personal data is owned by corporations. It may sound unnerving to think about how much our devices can learn about us, but in Web 3.0 there will never be a human on the other end of a device with access to our information. There will be no middleman businesses in charge of organizing our data before or after our devices use it. Plus, any time a device needs to send or share our personal data (to schedule a doctor's appointment for us, for example) it must ask for consent from us first. This consent-based data control will bring back the early decentralization of Web 1.0 and leave Big Data businesses behind in Web 2.0.

We're currently exploring the possibilities of Web 3.0 through the blockchain. Decentralized currency—otherwise known as cryptocurrency—is the most popular application of Web 3.0 possibilities. Blockchain developers have loftier goals than digital tokens for blockchain-based innovations. In later chapters, we'll explore how the blockchain can seamlessly transition us into the next phase of the Internet's cycle of improvement. Before we dive into the details of the blockchain, let's take a look at how the technology it uses will solve some of the most prominent issues we face on the Internet today.

CHAPTER 3

The Problems Blockchain Solves

In today's world, if a product or service claims to be free, it's because we're paying with our personal data. This might not sound like too big of a deal, but companies can use our personal data against us in some troubling ways. Far too often, people download free applications on their smartphones and tablets, completely unaware of what service providers are doing with their information behind the scenes.

When Sandy Clark's son came home from his first year of college, she wasn't used to him leaving the house without telling anyone when he would be back. She spent her nights awake until 2 AM, unable to sleep until she heard the soft click of the front door announcing her son's safe return. This pattern drained her energy and was unsustainable.

Sandy knew her son wasn't driving her insane with worry on purpose. College gave him a taste of independence, and when he came back home, he simply forgot to keep her in the loop about his plans. She didn't want her son to feel nagged or restricted every time she texted him, "Where are you?" or "When are you coming home?" But each night, she jumped out of her skin every time the phone rang, fearing a call from an officer who found her baby dead in a ditch somewhere.

After researching ways to ease her mind without restricting her son's freedom, she came across a free family safety app called Life360. The app would let her see her son's location and alert her when he left one location and arrived at another. She asked her son, her husband, and her younger daughter to download the app, and breathed a sigh of relief when they agreed. She thought she would finally be able to sleep easy again. However, that "free" app came at a hefty price, and when Sandy discovered what her family paid, she learned a critical lesson about how transactional relationships with Big Data companies cost more than we think.

Life360 promised that with a few simple taps on her phone, Sandy could locate her kids and see they were safe. The app tracked every user's real-time location, their battery life, when they were in a car, and the car's speed. Then, the data was relayed to family and friends in the user's "circle" so everyone could keep tabs on each other. Life360 offered her a passive path to peace of mind, and it didn't require her kids to tell her anything. It felt like a blessing...until Sandy's daughter discovered its curse.

Sandy's daughter was still in high school, and she'd heard about Life360 from some of her classmates. They all called it "creepy," but she didn't know why, so she read the fine print in the app's privacy policy. That's when she realized Life360 gave users' personal data to more than just their friends and family. In fact, the app was selling records of users' locations to anyone willing to pay for it.

Every time Sandy's phone pinged with her kids' location updates, another company received the same data.[7] When her daughter told her about Life360's sinister business model, she felt sick to her stomach. She couldn't believe an app that claimed to be "the #1 family safety app" would be so unsafe. She'd been worried about a police officer finding her son in a ditch, but now she pictured a sinister character *tracking* her son and *putting* him there. Sandy texted the rest of her family and told them to delete the app, bringing her back to square

---

[7] Keegan, John, and Alfred Ng. "Life360 Is Selling Precise Location Data on Its Tens of Millions of Users." The Markup, December 6, 2021. https://themarkup.org/privacy/2021/12/06/the-popular-family-safety-app-life360-is-selling-precise-location-data-on-its-tens-of-millions-of-user.

one. What would she do now? Without a safe solution to her problem, Sandy still couldn't sleep at night.

Then, Sandy came home the next day to find her children making dinner for the family. They sat down for a meal and talked about working together to bring their mom some peace. Her son suggested they make a groupchat and labeled it "Family Circle." With the dedicated chat, each family member could send in their plans for the day and what time they expected to be home. If they were late, in trouble, or changing plans, they could send in a little update for everyone to see. Sandy's son promised to communicate with his parents better and apologized for worrying them. And for the rest of his summer at home, he kept his promise. He even updated the Family Circle chat when he went back to school to keep up with the habit. Sandy never slept better.

Sandy, like many other moms who downloaded Life360, believed the app would help her keep her family safe. She didn't realize the cost for her peace of mind would be her family's privacy. Luckily, she discovered the hidden cost before anyone else used the data to put her family in danger. Life360 is an extreme example of a company selling data without directly informing its users, but it is only one of thousands of businesses that thrive by selling user data. In a world full of solutions to everyday problems, we're only given access to those solutions if we allow our personal information to be taken away from us. It feels like we've lost the ability to choose what happens to our data. Blockchain technology can give us back that choice.

Big Data, Big Problems

The internet has devolved into a mess of transactional relationships between users and businesses, but instead of paying with cash or credit, we're paying with our data. Our data includes personal information such as browser search histories, past purchases, people we communicated with, places we've visited, how much time we spend at certain places, and so much more. And when we use "free" apps, those apps usually are not free. We are relinquishing ownership of our data, and so what buyers do with it is out of our control.

Every time we swipe a credit card, send a tweet, or search the Internet, we create a new data point online. Each action we take online is added to a collection of data sets. These sets become so large that normal computing techniques can't process them. These collections, along with the frameworks, tools, and techniques businesses use to handle them, make up **Big Data**.

There has been a monumental increase in the data humans generate since the Internet became popular, and the amount we generate scales up constantly. From the beginning of recorded time all the way up to 2003, the entire world only had 5 billion gigabytes of data to store. In 2022, we will create about 3 billion gigabytes *per day*. If we were to store all the data we generate in a day on blu-ray disks, we would need 10 million of them, which would stack up to be as tall as four Eiffel Towers on top of one another.[8] The amount of data we create on a daily basis is expected to double every two years. For companies who want

---

[8]   Dihuni. "Every Day Big Data Statistics – 2.5 Quintillion Bytes of Data Created Daily." Dihuni. com: Digital Transformation Simplified, April 10, 2020. https://www.dihuni.com/2020/04/10/ every-day-big-data-statistics-2-5-quintillion-bytes-of-data-created-daily/.

the inside scoop on their consumers, Big Data provides a perfect (but bulky) solution.

We may not think about the data we generate until we see it manifest in unexpected ways. Our one-off, pure curiosity searches can cause some *weird* targeted ads to invade our online lives. One moment you look up "Marky Mark" because you remembered the Funky Bunch, and for the next week, you're flooded with ads for Calvin Klein's tighty whities.

The biggest names in the technology industry collect our data in exchange for the services they provide. When we sign up for new sites, services, or subscriptions, we're almost always greeted with a long, complicated Terms of Service popup. If we're being honest, most of us scroll straight to the "Accept" button without reading through what we're agreeing to. Buried deep in those Terms of Service in complex, messy language, is the company's caveat: you can use our service, but we're keeping track of every way you use it, and we have the right to use that information however we wish.

Facebook knows everything about its users. If you use Facebook, you've told them all about your likes, dislikes, friends, unfriends, and political affiliations. They know what you look like because they scan the photos you upload. They see what ads you click on, how long you look at a post, what times of day you scroll most...the list goes on. If you use Facebook, Instagram, or WhatsApp, their parent company, Meta, might know you better than you know yourself. Every time you log in, you share parts of yourself with a giant corporation.

Google's parent company, Alphabet, doesn't catch as much flack in the news as Meta does, but they collect the same amount of data from their users, if not more. Even their most seemingly-innocent applications are a treasure trove for user data. If you've ever used Google Photos to store backups of your pictures, in the fine print, you've given up ownership of those photos. Google can access your albums and do whatever they want with the pictures. They claim the data is only used to "scan photos for advertising opportunities," but if they change their mind, there's nothing we can do about it. We already signed on the digital dotted line.

It might be scary to think about, but even GPS apps like Google Maps, Apple Maps, and Waze collect our data and sell it to third parties.[9] These businesses know their service is more convenient to users than trying to hold a map wider than the windshield while they're driving, but that convenience comes at a cost. While we follow GPS routes, the app collects data like where we live, where we travel most, and how long we are regularly away from home.

Now, most of the third parties purchasing our data only use it to sell their products or services to us. If we regularly stop at a Starbucks on our way to work, third parties know we're big coffee drinkers. If our entire digital photo album is pictures of our kids, they can deliver ads for diapers, babysitters, and kids toys. The more we click on Facebook ads, the more these third parties know their marketing is working. However, these businesses aren't collecting our data to throw it away once they've used it. They're collecting it and storing it—and it's not always stored safely.

Meta, formerly known as Facebook Inc., has seen major data breaches that not only exposed its users, but revealed how much data Facebook actually collected from them. In 2018, a British Consulting Firm created a third-party quiz app that sneakily scraped and sold data from around 90 million Facebook users. In 2019, a cyber risk team discovered 540 million user data records—including emails, passwords, user comments, and user likes—leaked from a few of Facebook's third-party app developers. In 2021, another 530 million Facebook users had their data exposed by hackers who released full names, phone numbers, and passwords. Facebook has been fined multiple times for their insufficient security measures, but little is expected to change. The massive amounts of data the company collects will always make them a target for Big Data thieves.

---

[9]   Tallent, Amanda. "What Personal Data Do Navigation Apps Collect?" MarkTechPost, July 12, 2019. https://www.marktechpost.com/2019/07/12/what-personal-data-do-navigation-apps-collect/.

Most companies that store Big Data today put our data at risk by storing it in a **centralized** location. Centralized locations exist in one place or are controlled by one person or authority. A bank vault is an example of a centralized location used to store money. However, when a bank robber wants to break in, he knows exactly where the money is kept. Once he assembles a team and gets his hands on a map of the bank, it's only a matter of time before he breaks through, and then everything inside is his for the taking. The same is true for our data when businesses store it on a single computer. Even a centralized network requires all of the computers to communicate by passing through a single authority, so all a hacker needs to do is remove the authority to bring down the whole system. As long as businesses store Big Data with centralization, Big Data puts us all in danger of online attacks.

Since the Internet's popularization, we as users have grown more wary of possible online attacks. Most businesses have their employees complete training on internet safety as part of their onboarding process. Parents give talks to their children about strong passwords and strict privacy settings before making new accounts online. Email platforms have stronger filters to prevent users from clicking attacks disguised as legitimate messages. We've gotten better at recognizing when we're being played online, but while we're busy deciding whether to trust an online purchase, an entire industry is capitalizing on our technology trust issues.

Monetizing Trust

Our lack of control over our personal data is worsening by the day. Traveling through the Internet without a keen eye for scammers and hackers is as dangerous today as it was to take a moonlight stroll through the woods in the time of Little Red Riding Hood. Understandably, that makes users nervous. Some businesses recognized users' growing fear of the Internet and decided to offer their services as a middleman. They hold out their hand and offer to guide people through some of the Internet's most treacherous transactions. Most of us accept the deal.

These **middleman businesses** act as a go-between for us, the customers, and the goods or services we want to purchase and/or access. Middleman businesses promise us they've got our backs if our transaction goes wrong, but they don't hand out trust for free. Most make a pretty penny in service fees, commissions, and your sweet, sweet data.

Once customers grew tired of being scammed every time they bought a new table (I'm looking at you, Craigslist) they turned to middleman businesses for trusted transactions. Companies like eBay, Amazon, and Etsy are the most popular middleman businesses for products. They provide a platform for independent sellers to offer their goods, and they act as a middleman between sellers and customers. If a product from a seller goes missing, if the money doesn't make it from customer to seller, or if a dispute breaks out between the two ends of the transaction, these middlemen jump in and save the day. Customers appreciate the extra backup when a transaction goes wrong, but not all of them realize these middlemen are collecting cash *and* data from both sides of every transaction.

Some middleman businesses provide a trusted go-between for services that could be dangerous without them. It might seem reckless to hop in any old car and ask for a ride, so Uber and Lyft act as the middleman between riders and drivers. They conduct background checks on their drivers and offer support if a ride goes wrong. AirBnB, VRBO, and other vacation rental businesses make it safer to shack up in a stranger's home for a few nights. In exchange for their safety checks, these middleman businesses pocket a portion of every transaction they stand between.

Even banks, the most basic, common businesses for money management, are middlemen between the average consumer and their money. Banks use centralized storage to secure our banking information, which makes even a simple task like wiring money complicated and time-consuming. This becomes especially difficult when transferring money from one country to another, where exchange rates vary between banks and brokers. The transfers rack up transaction fees and long processing times with every middleman they pass through. Your data is shared with every middleman along the way, and each one stores it in a centralized system. Then, when a bank or a middleman suffers an attack on their centralized storage systems, the security breaches are devastating.

There are even middleman businesses that exist solely to guard personal information from breaches, and they go so far as to keep it from the person the information is about. Data brokers, like Equifax, scrape customer data like financial transfers, social media activity, browsing history, location data, and more to generate a huge profit off of their "customers." Then, they sell the information right back to the customers, as if their data never belonged to them. Equifax holds a ledger of your personal data, but they're not letting you see what's inside for free. They're keeping it tucked away on a centralized storage system, safe and sound...until it's not.

Although middlemen businesses monetize the trust of their customers, not all of them are worthy. In 2017, Equifax's centralized storage system was breached. As a result, personally identifying information for 143 million people—more than 40 percent of the United States— was exposed.[10] Names, addresses, dates of birth, Social Security numbers, and even drivers' licenses numbers were leaked to the public. Some users who paid Equifax to see their own credit report had the misfortune of adding their credit card number to their list of exposed data. Most victims of the breach didn't realize Equifax stored any of their information to begin with, much less in such a vulnerable place.

We're used to trusting middleman businesses to provide us with trusted transactions. Many of us have never lived in a world without middlemen to guide us along. Data breaches feel like a risk we have no choice to accept, because we don't know how to conduct all the small transactions we complete on a daily basis by ourselves. But what if there was another way?

---

[10] Fruhlinger, Josh. "Equifax Data Breach FAQ: What Happened, Who Was Affected, What Was the Impact?" CSO Online. CSO, February 12, 2020. https://www.csoonline.com/article/3444488/equifax-data-breach-faq-what-happened-who-was-affected-what-was-the-impact.html.

Taking Back Control

In the years before blockchain technology, some Internet users went rogue to outsmart Big Data and the middleman businesses we see everywhere today. Morgan Sung, a journalist in her mid-twenties, grew tired of seeing ads for diapers, baby bottles, and teething toys simply because she was a young woman.[11] She decided to cheat the system by releasing a Kraken into her personal data stream.

After six months of carefully curating her clicks, all of her accounts were jam-packed with ads for kraken-themed home decor. Amazon advertised a teapot with an octopus tentacle for a handle. Walmart offered her an end table shaped like an octopus holding a piece of glass. An octopus chandelier from Overstock showed up on her Facebook feed. Her goal was to mess with the algorithms that claimed to know her so well by giving them the digital middle finger.

When the blockchain first appeared, it offered promising solutions for Internet users like Morgan Sung who want more control over their online presence. Blockchain technology offers alternatives for people who don't want their data collected and sold to the highest bidder every time they visit a new website. It also poses a huge threat to the entire middleman industry by offering a new way for people to interact, whether they're exchanging goods, services, money, or messages.

The blockchain enables **peer-to-peer** (P2P) transactions, which allows one user to transfer information to another without the need for a middleman. In the blockchain, every P2P transaction becomes public, which means any interested party can view and verify the details. Public doesn't mean your credit card number is on display—it means when you sell your car to Joe, you don't need to post it on a middleman car-buying website like Carvana and wait for Joe to buy it from them. You can sell your car to Joe directly, and your transaction becomes public information. Joe can't say, "I gave her the money but I never got

---

[11]   Sung, Morgan. "It Turns Out Purposely Messing With Your Targeted Ads Isn't a Good Idea." Mashable. Mashable, April 26, 2019. https://mashable.com/article/purposely-engaging-with-weird-ads-isnt-good.

the car!" because the information is readily available to anyone who looks for it.

Information stored on the blockchain exists in a **decentralized** system, which makes your personal data much more difficult to steal because it isn't all kept in one place. Instead of storing data on a single server, the blockchain splits up its storage across dozens, hundreds, sometimes thousands of different locations. Combine this with the complex technological processes the blockchain uses to hide your data (we'll get into that later), and you can control who accesses your information and how it is used.

Once blockchains become the default framework behind how we use the Internet, users can take back control of their data. In a world where an online presence isn't optional if we want to be functioning members of society, this technology will allow us to regain our digital freedom. But before we can see the ways the blockchain will revolutionize our everyday life, we must understand what the blockchain is and how it works.

CHAPTER 4

The Basics of Blockchain

Web 3.0's promising future wouldn't be possible without blockchain technology. Like the Internet, the blockchain is also experiencing a cycle of improvement. This one is moving a little faster—which makes sense, since Internet developers didn't have the Internet to help them along.

The attractive aspects of blockchain lie in its decentralization, cryptography, and trustless peer-to-peer (P2P) transaction capability. In this chapter, we'll dive deeper into these terms and more to build a foundational understanding of the blockchain. Then, we'll build on our foundation to explore the blockchain's implications for our future. But first, an analogy.

A long, long time ago, before smartphones, automobiles, and indoor plumbing, ten families came together and formed a village. These villagers worked together to grow their community. They hunted, gathered, raised children and animals, and traded their goods with each other. The hunter traded meat with the farmer for rice. The baker gave bread to the caregiver, and in exchange she watched his children during the day. The doctor traded medicine for clothes with the tailor. This system worked fine, but every so often, the villagers needed to take out an advance.

"Today was a bad hunting day," the hunter said to the farmer, "but if you give me some rice now, I promise to give you meat from my next hunt."

The farmer agreed because he trusted the hunter. Then, the tailor asked for rice before the farmer's new clothes were finished. The baker needed wheat and couldn't offer bread without it. After a few months of this, more and more promises were made across the village, and they became difficult to track. The villagers argued over promises forgotten or never made at all. The village's economy came to a screeching halt, and none of the villagers trusted each other anymore. They needed a solution before they either starved or attacked one another with the farmer's pitchforks.

The villagers came together and decided to appoint one member to keep track of all the promises they made. They called him the Ledgerman. The man they chose was unusually small and slender. He had a handlebar mustache, a jagged scar down his cheek, and a blood red eyepatch.

"He seems trustworthy!" The villagers decided.

The Ledgerman got to work tracking promises. Trades moved smoothly again for a little while. The hunter could promise meat to the farmer, then the two could meet the Ledgerman to consolidate their payment. Now, the villagers didn't need to trust each other—they only needed to trust the Ledgerman.

The Ledgerman became a vital part of the village's economy, but the power proved too tempting for him. One day, the Ledgerman announced he wanted a small fee for every trade he recorded. He didn't have time to bake bread or sow fields with all this ledger tracking going on. The villagers weren't thrilled about losing out on some of their profits, but no one wanted to bring it up to the Ledgerman. (He had a surprisingly creepy stare for a guy with one eye.) The villagers had no choice but to take his deal.

Ledgerman accumulated wealth and power with his new source of income. He took bribes to change the ledger when villagers wanted more out of their trades. He *gave* bribes to villagers to keep his position as the Ledgerman. He raised his fees whenever he felt like it. He figured because he played such a crucial role to the villagers, there wasn't anything they could do to stop him.

The villagers sometimes voiced their anger with the Ledgerman, but they knew they needed him to keep their trades running. Every time a villager complained, the Ledgerman shrugged his shoulders, twisted his mustache between his fingers, and made a little note in the ledger. The next time that villager went to make a trade, the fees climbed higher. Many of the villagers felt defeated by the very system they'd built.

One afternoon, the baker's anger came to a head. He tried to make a trade for meat, but the Ledgerman's fees were more expensive than the trade itself! The baker erupted into a ball of flying fists and spit-filled shouts. His fury was contagious, and soon the square filled with angry villagers screaming at the Ledgerman. Afraid for his life, the Ledgerman fled the town with his ledger tucked under his arm.

The villagers came together to find a new solution to their problem. They liked the idea of a ledger, but no one wanted to be the new Ledgerman. Everyone knew the responsibility was too much for one person to handle. As they brainstormed new ways to record their trades, the caregiver proposed a brilliant new system.

"Why don't all of us keep a ledger?"

The village loved the idea. Twice a day, one villager from each family met up in the square to make trades and track them in their ledgers. Every promise was recorded in every family's ledger. Then, once a week, the villagers met again to hold "Village Validation Day." Here, each family member read off their ledger and cross-checked it with the others.

In one meeting, the farmer recorded a promise to deliver five bags of rice to the hunter. However, the hunter recorded that he was owed ten bags. The two started arguing over which entry was the right one.

"Why don't you trust me?" the farmer hollered, "I don't even have a mustache!"

"Why don't *you* trust *me*?" the hunter hollered back, "I've never used an eyepatch!"

The caregiver stepped forward and reminded the arguing villagers they didn't need to trust each other. Thanks to their new, trustless system, every villager's ledger recorded the trade. They simply had to cross-check the other ledgers and see which promise—five bags or ten—was recorded the most. The villagers lined up to read their records, forming a chain across the square.

What are Blockchains?

Blockchains are a type of **Distributed Ledger Technology (DLT),** which refers to any decentralized database that records, validates, and stores information in an unchangeable way.[12] Instead of storing all information in a centralized location, a blockchain spreads its ledger across multiple machines. The computers that host a blockchain's ledger together are the nodes. Unlike centralized systems, nodes in a blockchain don't need a central server to act as a middleman when they communicate with each other. Nodes communicate to consistently update the blockchain they host.

---

[12] Frankenfield, Jake. "Distributed Ledger Technology." Investopedia. Investopedia, February 8, 2022. https://www.investopedia.com/terms/d/distributed-ledger-technology-dlt.asp.

Centralized

Decentralized

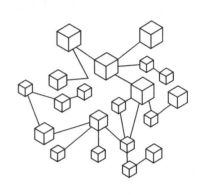

Distributed Ledger Technology

Decentralization is a critical component of blockchain technology. Blockchains are decentralized both politically and architecturally.[13] By preventing any one person, company, or group from controlling the information hosted on a public blockchain, the integrity of the information is much more secure. Power outages, political turmoil, and malicious attacks can't bring down a system that is equally distributed across multiple machines. By spreading the information across multiple machines, the blockchain does not have a single point of failure.

To understand the security of a blockchain, it helps to envision its base components as literal chains and blocks. A **blockchain** is a digital ledger made up of a chain of blocks. **Blocks** are packages or structures that store information as data. Blocks can contain data about almost anything: transactions, assets, tracking information, and more. The first block on a chain is called the **Genesis Block**, and it contains the original data that other blocks build from. Each block on the blockchain is reliant on the one before.

13   Waldman, Jonathan. Blockchain - Blockchain Fundamentals. Microsoft Docs, March 2018. https://docs.microsoft.com/en-us/archive/msdn-magazine/2018/march/blockchain-blockchain-fundamentals.

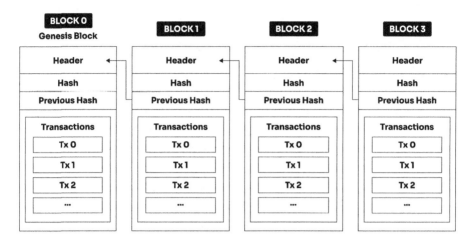

The structure of a block in blockchain

Once a new block is added to the chain, the block can't be changed, hacked, or cheated without disrupting the entire chain. This makes blockchains **immutable.** If a hacker wanted to corrupt data stored in a blockchain, they would have to change every block that came before it on the chain. This makes it impossible to tamper with blockchains without anyone noticing. As blockchains grow and new blocks are added, the security of the blockchain as a whole improves.

The public structure of a blockchain is what allows the technology to be trustless. The terms "trust" and "trustless" aren't opposites when we're talking about blockchain tech. "Trust" refers to the faith users place in a third party, especially banks. Most people in the U.S. are comfortable storing their money with banks. Most of us don't question that our medical records are stored at the doctor's office. When we need a copy of a high school or college transcript, we trust the school to keep those records in storage. We don't consider how much trust we place in single entities when it comes to our personal, vital information.

Blockchains are "**trustless**" because they store information without requiring users to place any trust in a third party.[14] Trustless systems

---

[14] Cryptopedia Staff. "Trustless Blockchains and Non-Custodial Wallets." Cryptopedia. Cryptopedia, August 11, 2021. https://www.gemini.com/cryptopedia/ trustless-meaning-blockchain-non-custodial-smart-contracts.

aren't shady or unworthy of trust, but they don't rely on trust to do their job. Instead of asking users to rely on a single stranger, middleman business, or institution, the blockchain proves itself worthy of trust through computer code. Blockchain users place their trust in the process of their transactions, not the entity they're transacting through. The blockchain anticipates its users saying, *You think you're so great? Prove it!*

Blockchain technology maintains its trustlessness in three ways. First, the nature of the blockchain prevents anyone from altering, removing, or adding data to a block once it's added to the chain. **Cryptography** in blockchain technology involves scrambling the original content of a message to a cipher before sending it to the recipient, and only the recipient can unscramble the message by using a combination of cryptographic keys. This way, no other parties can intercept a message and alter it.

Second, blockchains maintain access with **cryptographic keys**. These keys are a string of letters and numbers that point to an address—or wallet—in a blockchain. There are two types of cryptographic keys: a public key and a private key. A **public key** allows others to view information on the blockchain. A **private key** allows a user to enact transactions, view their information, or make updates to it. A public key is like your username—others can use it to search for your profile on social media. It may not be your real name, but it is a unique identifier to you. (Public keys are random, so think: A2C7UBV29C1 and not: BlockchainBoss69.) People who look up your username can read your profile, but they can't make changes unless they log into your account with a password. The private key acts as your password, protecting the details within your blockchain account.

IMPORTANT: NEVER give your private key to anyone. NEVER EVER.

Every blockchain user has one of each of the cryptographic keys, and each node on the blockchain has access to them. The nodes use encrypted, mathematical equations to create a digital signature out of the public and private keys. Users can authorize their activity on the blockchain with their digital signature.

The third way blockchains remain trustless is, ironically, by relying on users to manage the system themselves. Without third parties to mediate interactions, users can interact with each other directly through peer-to-peer collaboration.

Peer-to-peer (P2P) transactions replace middlemen in blockchain technology. In P2P environments, decisions are made democratically. Participants within the blockchain come to a **consensus,** meaning at least 51 percent of them must agree, before any decisions can be made. It doesn't matter if some of the blockchain participants are mustache-twisting, eyepatch-wearing, Slenderman-looking villains, because their evil plans can't pass without a majority vote. None of the participants are required to trust each other because none of them make decisions independently. In essence, P2P transactions function the same way the villagers traded in The Village Story once they defeated the Ledgerman.

Every Village Validation Day, the villagers compared their ledger entries with one another. When the entries matched, the ledgers were in consensus. Sometimes, though, there were entries that didn't match.

The hunter and farmer were arguing about two different entries in their ledgers. The farmer believed he only promised the hunter five bags of rice, but the hunter recorded ten bags in his ledger. Which promise was correct? Who should be trusted?

The beauty of the village's system was that neither needed to be trusted to find out the truth. The other villagers all read out their entries about the same promise. Three entries said the farmer owed ten bags, while seven said he only promised five. The tally brought the group into consensus and the villagers all updated their ledgers accordingly.

The villagers accomplished the same goal as the earliest iterations of the blockchain. They removed the middleman—the sinister

Ledgerman—and eliminated the fees he brought with him. They created a trustless system by using a P2P system with decentralized ledgers. Over time, though, the villagers ran into issues with scalability and security as other families joined their community. But like the blockchain, their system evolved to overcome new struggles.

A Brief History of Blockchain

The details of the blockchain's evolution are hotly debated in the tech industry. Some people believe the first blockchain appeared in the early 90s, while others firmly believe blockchains didn't exist before Bitcoin. Some experts claim we're entering the Blockchain 3.0 stage now, in 2022, while others think Blockchain 3.0 is actually Blockchain 1.0 because the technology hasn't evolved enough for an official new version. Others claim we're really operating in Blockchain 5.0. Like the Internet, it'll probably be decades before we can zoom out far enough to see clear distinctions between the blockchain's phases.

The history of the blockchain is less of a straight line and more of a loop-de-loop. Different blockchain features are all growing at the same time, bending around and twisting with each other like two ends of a soft pretzel. Some blockchain applications look like simple salted pretzels, fully realized with all that Blockchain 1.0 has to offer. Other applications need complimentary blockchain features, like pretzels need mustard or nacho cheese, to be fully satisfying. Future blockchain possibilities are still waiting to launch on Blockchain 3.0, like a fresh batch of soft pretzels waiting for the stand to open for business. (Are you hungry yet?)

The timeline in this section describes, combines, or ignores some of these theories and speculations to lay out the broad strokes of the blockchain's evolution. The dates associated with each phase of the blockchain exist to point out when the phases first appeared. We'll likely see improvements in all three versions of blockchain technology in the future.

1991–2014: Blockchain 1.0: Cryptocurrency

Blockchain started in 1991 as a simple process to protect timestamps on Word documents. Scientists Stuart Haber and W. Scott Stornetta built a secure chain of blocks in a work titled "How to time-stamp a digital document." The next year, the two improved their technology to store multiple documents in a single block, increasing blockchain efficiency.

The introduction of Merkle trees brought the blockchain to a new level. **Merkle trees** are data structures divided into layers. The layers are organized by a single root in the block, and all the nodes in the layers are associated with the root. With this organization, Merkle trees enable blockchain technology to verify and store bigger collections of data within a single block.

The next development in blockchain technology arrived in 2002, when the concept for decentralized trust within a network file system popped up. Then, in 2005, an early concept for cryptocurrency called Bitgold flashed across financial headlines. But these systems only toyed with the concept of the blockchain. Its inception came later in 2008, when Satoshi Nakamoto created the first functioning blockchain and paired it with an exciting application.

Satoshi Nakamoto is widely considered to be the brains behind the blockchain we know today. Nakamoto might be a man, or a woman, or a group of men and women. No one knows the identity behind the name. All we know is that he (or she, or they) created Bitcoin, the world's first cryptocurrency *and* the first practical application of blockchain technology.

In 2009, many countries were reeling from the U.S. financial crisis. It's no coincidence that the blockchain's revolutionary technology appeared right after one of the biggest economic disruptions in recent history. Nakamoto published a white paper, *Bitcoin: A Peer-to-Peer Electronic*

Cash System, that detailed Bitcoin and its underlying technology.[15] Nakamoto believed Bitcoin and the blockchain, if used correctly, could eliminate the need for single-party control in the financial system. After big banks failed to support their clients, Nakamoto proposed a system to eliminate them from the financial process altogether. The abstract succinctly describes the goal of Bitcoin:

A purely peer-to-peer version of electronic cash would allow online payments to be sent directly from one party to another without going through a financial institution.

Bitcoin's blockchain relied on a type of consensus algorithm to replace the need for third parties in its transactions. Nakamoto presented the concept of **Proof-of-Work** (PoW), a consensus process for verifying transactions with computing power. As Bitcoin grew, so did its demands for electricity and computer power, which presented real-world consequences for digital-world money. However, PoW made Bitcoin more robust, trustless, and efficient than any other technology of its time. It's still considered the glue that holds Bitcoin together.

Nakamoto was the first person (or people) to use Bitcoin's blockchain. Programmer Hal Finney received ten Bitcoin from Nakamoto as a reward for helping build the system. The transaction is documented in Bitcoin's Genesis Block:

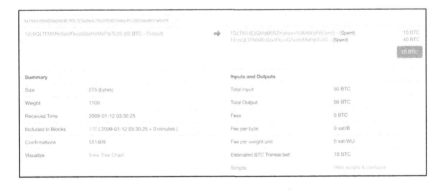

---

[15]   Nakamoto, Satoshi. "Bitcoin: A Peer-to-Peer Electronic Cash System." Bitcoin.org, October 31, 2008. https://bitcoin.org/bitcoin.pdf.

In the transaction, we see the public keys for each account across the top of the report. The time, amount, and size of the transaction are also recorded. In today's world, most Bitcoin transactions have small fees attached and account addresses are displayed differently. Bitcoin has made plenty of innovations since their first official transaction took place, but those will be discussed in a later chapter.

From 2009 to 2014, Bitcoin's stake as the only cryptocurrency made its popularity grow. Blockchain innovation—especially in the cryptocurrency industry—gathered attention from all kinds of people. In 2010, Nakamoto vanished without a trace, leaving Bitcoin to a handful of developers. The Father of Decentralized Finance (**DeFi**) vanished without ever taking credit for revolutionizing the technology industry.

The rise of Bitcoin inspired other cryptocurrencies to appear over the next few years. Today, there are over 3400 kinds of cryptocurrency, each with their own take on blockchain technology. Bitcoin's biggest successor came one year later, when one of its contributors branched off to write a bigger, better blockchain.

2014-2018: Blockchain 2.0: Dapps & Smart Contracts

Vitalik Buterin worked for Bitcoin during its early stages, but he believed he could improve on Nakamoto's idea. Buterin split from Bitcoin and wrote a new blockchain in 2015 called Ethereum. While Ethereum began as another framework to run the cryptocurrency Ether (ETH), it left room for additional improvements to blockchain technology.

Ethereum introduced two new concepts to the blockchain. The first was the ability to execute decentralized apps (also called **dapps**) on a blockchain. This innovation opened the door for new business applications. Industries outside of finance could use the blockchain's decentralized, trustless, P2P functionality without diving into the confusing world of cryptocurrency.

The second concept Ethereum introduced was **Smart Contracts.** These simple computer programs automatically facilitate transactions between two parties on the blockchain when certain terms are met. Smart contracts allow the exchange of money, shares, property, or any other asset. Once a smart contract is executed on the blockchain, it can't be canceled, erased, or changed. They also remove the biggest point of failure for traditional contracts: human interpretation. Smart contracts leave no room for loopholes or breaches in trust.

Smart contracts simplify transactions that don't take place in real time. If a company hires a web developer with a smart contract to design their website, they can set the terms of the deal in advance. If they set a deal to pay upon delivery, the developer doesn't receive payment until the company receives the product. Once the smart contract program verifies that the product was delivered and meets all of the requirements, the developer is automatically paid. The company can't turn around and argue about the website's quality, and the developer can't ask for payment before delivery.

Smart contracts can apply to more than financial agreements. Libraries can use smart contracts to lend or take back copies of their e-books by setting date ranges for rentals. Insurance companies can program smart contracts to trigger automatic payouts when a flight is delayed, a hurricane strikes, or a stock crashes. A smart contract for someone with high blood pressure can link to the Health app on their Smart Watch and call 911 if their blood pressure spikes to dangerous levels. The technology behind smart contracts is simple enough to leave room for an infinite number of possibilities.

Ethereum's capability to host dapps and execute smart contracts made it the go-to blockchain for **Non-Fungible Tokens** (NFTs).[16] NFTs are digital assets that contain identifying information recorded in smart contracts. They can represent tangible items, like a concert ticket, or intangible items, like a special item in a video game. These tokens are

---

[16] Hamilton, A. "The Beginning of NFTs - A Brief History of NFT Art." Zeno Fine Art. Zeno Fine Art, March 3, 2022. https://www.zenofineart.com/blogs/news/ the-beginning-of-nfts-a-brief-history-of-nft-art.

considered non-fungible because they cannot be duplicated, divided, or exchanged like-for-like.

Bitcoin, Ether, and other cryptocurrencies are fungible tokens. If a user sends her friend one Bitcoin and he sends it back, she still has one Bitcoin. She can also send a friend smaller amounts of one Bitcoin, measured in **satoshis** (thanks, Nakamoto!) like cents measure amounts smaller than one U.S. dollar.

NFTs are like snowflakes because no two are identical. If two users traded NFT concert tickets, they don't end the transaction with the same value they started with. Even if both NFTs were for the same concert on the same night, the value still wouldn't be the same, because each NFT corresponds to a different seat. They also can't trade part of their NFT for the same reason they couldn't trade half of a paper concert ticket—it wouldn't be worth anything on its own and wouldn't be redeemable.[17]

Ethereum became the second most popular blockchain within months of its first appearance. The founders welcomed new startups to design dapps and use their smart contract capabilities. Blockchain 2.0 brought the technology's status from niche to emerging, and thousands of companies built blockchain-based solutions to revolutionize their business. But as the future possibilities for blockchains were tested, a few critical weaknesses appeared.

2018-Present: Blockchain 3.0: Enterprise

As blockchain technology expanded at an exponential pace, issues with its capabilities and deficiencies emerged. Scalability and security became more complicated to manage. The more users joined Blockchain 1.0's Bitcoin, the more difficult it became to authorize and validate transactions quickly enough through PoW. It wasn't an issue when a few hundred people used the blockchain, but with millions of users

---

[17] Melanie Kramer, Stephen Graves. "Beginner's Guide to NFTs: What Are Non-Fungible Tokens?" Decrypt. Decrypt, January 18, 2022. https://decrypt.co/resources/non-fungible-tokens-nfts-explained-guide-learn-blockchain.

trading Bitcoin all the time, those transactions backed up and created a bottleneck. Bitcoin's blockchain verified at about seven transactions per second. Meanwhile, Visa processes 2,000 credit card transactions per second.[18] Older blockchains became bloated, inefficient, and outdated. It wasn't long before sending a Bitcoin transaction would've been easier through snail mail! Businesses needed solutions to avoid disappearing altogether from the industry they created.

Blockchain 3.0 is a blanket term describing the industry's shift to solving glaring problems with previous versions. Instead of developing dapps to integrate with existing blockchains like Ethereum, many businesses are designing their own blockchains. These new blockchains are replacing PoW with more energy-efficient consensus mechanisms. In addition to solving blockchain's toughest challenges, the new version of blockchain is building to improve its capabilities. Overall, Blockchain 3.0 is meant to expand and improve the technology to achieve global adoption.

It's likely that the first time you heard about the blockchain fell somewhere on Blockchain 3.0's spot on the timeline. This period is when blockchains moved beyond decentralized financial solutions to improve the storage and transfer of sensitive data. Better processes for scalability, security, and decentralization are appearing every day, making the blockchain a promising application for future enterprises. By the time Blockchain 4.0 emerges, it's likely that the technology will already be part of everyday life.

---

[18] Bybit Learn. "Blockchain 3.0." Bybit Learn. Bybit, May 13, 2022. https://learn.bybit.com/glossary/definition-blockchain-3.0/.

CHAPTER 5

How Does the Blockchain Work?

On January 3, 2009 at 1:15 PM EST, Satoshi Nakamoto tucked the mission statement for Bitcoin inside the first block on the blockchain. Unlike the millions of blocks that came after its release, Bitcoin's Genesis Block contained a message in its code.

> The Times 03/Jan/2009 Chancellor on Brink of Second
> Bailout for Banks

This headline from the London Times which describes an article about the British government bailing out a big bank. It's not common for blocks on the chain to contain secret messages, but Nakamoto wanted to make a point as loud and clear as possible. Many Bitcoin fans have interpreted this message as the thesis for what Bitcoin, and therefore cryptocurrency in general, is all about: cut out the banks. By cutting out banks—the middlemen in financial transactions—there will no longer be a need for governments to give these corporations seemingly unlimited financial mercy that is not shown to citizens.

Bitcoin can't be bailed out, nor would it ever need to be bailed out, because it has no central agency. There is no middleman. No third party to cash a government bailout check. If the government came knocking on Bitcoin's door, there would be no big, brawny banker there to answer. Thus, Bitcoin became known as "The People's Currency" because it allows anyone, anywhere to directly interact with their money. No one needs a bank account or even a government ID to make money with Bitcoin. No transactions can bounce, on purpose or on accident, which lends trust to the system. Transparent transaction details settle disputes and discourage conmen and cheats.

Bitcoin set the bar high for blockchain technology. People loved the idea of a system with no nefarious authorities, no secret sales, and no middlemen twisting their mustaches while skimming off the top of transactions. They loved it so much, in fact, that they wanted the technology for more than just financial purposes. The question had to be asked, what other unnecessary middlemen can we cut out? Can we create a fully democratic system on the blockchain?

A democratic system that is still secure, transparent, and trustworthy is a tall order. To go about creating this revolutionary system, blockchain builders wove together complex features and processes. They expanded the framework to apply to more than financial transactions. Today, builders are continuing to build on the framework as new applications appear. But before we explore new use cases, we must understand how blockchains accomplish their lofty goals.

Types of Blockchains

Although the last chapter defined all blockchains as decentralized, this is really an umbrella term. Blockchains come in all shapes, sizes, and levels of centralization. They can be public, private, or a combination of the two. These are the four most common types of blockchain.

Public: Public blockchains are entirely decentralized. They are completely transparent, meaning anyone can view their information, and they are completely independent of any organization, so they're resistant to business closures and corruption. Public blockchains are also pseudo-anonymous, meaning users can join in with a pseudonym that doesn't identify them to others. Bitcoin popularized this kind of blockchain, and today, most cryptocurrencies exist on public blockchains.

Public blockchains tend to run slower than the others because they have more nodes in their network. Since all nodes must give consensus, public blockchains take more time to carry out actions. Imagine deciding on dinner plans—it's hard enough for two people to agree, now add 10,000 more! More nodes make public blockchains more secure, but it also makes their processing time for transactions longer. Their scalability is a problem blockchain builders are still trying to solve.

Private: Private blockchains are similar to public blockchains, except they are controlled by a single organization. Private blockchains—also called permissioned—still use P2P connections, and they might be stored across multiple nodes, but each node is still under one controlling authority.

The controlling authority in private blockchains is less like a big banker and more like a big bouncer. Private blockchains are restricted to only allow certain people in, so access to private information is limited. Large institutions, like banks, could benefit from private blockchains because they could store their clients' financial information and share it between branches without allowing public access.

Private blockchains are most common for businesses because they provide fast, secure data storage without public access. However, because their number of nodes is limited to the size of their network, private blockchains tend to be less secure. The fewer nodes on a network, the easier it is for hackers to break in.

Hybrid: Some organizations want the best of both worlds—benefits from public and private blockchains. Hybrid blockchains allow companies to set up a permissions-based blockchain alongside a public blockchain. Then, they can control which information is publicly accessible and which is stored in a private section. Transactions on a hybrid blockchain are typically not made public, but they can allow verification when needed. Access to the transaction can be gained through smart contracts. The medical field benefits from hybrid blockchains because they block third parties from accessing patient medical records, but users can access and verify their own information through a smart contract.

Consortium: Also known as a federated blockchain, consortium blockchains are similar to hybrid blockchains because they use features of both public and private blockchains. In consortium blockchains, though, multiple organizations can collaborate across a decentralized network. These networks prevent a single authority from controlling the blockchain while still remaining private. For example, IBM Food Trust is a private blockchain that allows businesses on the food supply chain to track their products from harvest to customer purchase. Only IBM Food Trust employees and their partner companies have access to their blockchain. Consortium blockchains work like a sort of digital relationship—IBM can't kick their partners out after a fight, and no party can invite a third without permission from everyone else.

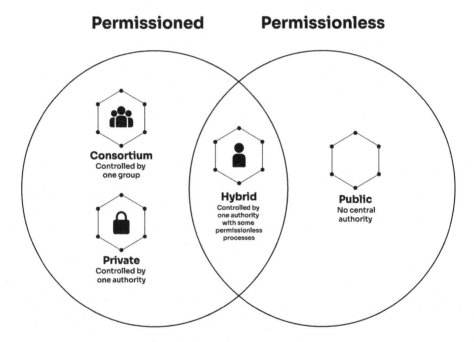

Permissioned   Permissionless

Consortium
Controlled by
one group

Hybrid
Controlled by
one authority
with some
permissionless
processes

Public
No central
authority

Private
Controlled by
one authority

Types of blockchain

Each blockchain type has its own positive and negative features, and industries looking to use the technology can take their pick based on what works best for them. Trading networks like cryptocurrencies,

NFTs, and online marketplaces are best on public blockchains for their trusted transaction visibility. Real estate agencies may choose a hybrid blockchain to show their listings to the public while protecting their clients' personal information. Private companies like Walmart can use private blockchains to monitor their supply chains. If companies need to securely share data, like insurance companies and medical centers, they can do it on a consortium blockchain.

Core Components of the Blockchain

Although each type of blockchain functions a little differently, there are a few core components that make all of them work. Whether a blockchain is public, private, or a combination of the two, its network has a version of these core components. Each core component is like its own individual color on the Color Wheel; combining them in different ways creates thousands of technological applications. For the sake of simplicity, we're only going to cover how each color is used to create the full, technicolor picture of the blockchain.

Ledger: The ledger is the database of recorded information that makes up the blockchain. The traditional ledgers most of us are familiar with are single copies of information in leather notebooks. Distributed ledgers, where copies of the information exist in multiple places, appeared with shared documents in programs like Google Docs and Microsoft OneDrive. In blockchains, the ledger is both distributed and decentralized, which means each computer (node) in the blockchain network holds equal control over the ledger's information. Every computer works together with the others to maintain the ledger accurately and securely.

Nodes: Nodes are the machines that host the blockchain's ledger. Full Nodes maintain a full copy of the ledger and have the ability to validate, accept, and reject blockchain transactions. Partial Nodes, or Lightweight Nodes, don't hold full copies, but they maintain a hash value (see below). These nodes still contribute to the blockchain's security, but their low computational power and low storage make them limited.

Wallet: Like a leather, plastic, or duct tape wallet, a digital wallet on the blockchain allows its owner to store data (in most cases, cryptocurrency and NFTs). Public and private keys attached to the wallets—not physically, like a chunky keychain, but digitally—allow users to stay anonymous when they make transactions on the blockchain. While wallets only exist to store and exchange digital assets right now, their frameworks could prove useful to build other storage options on the blockchain in the future.

Hash: Hashes are the backbone of a blockchain network. All blocks on the chain are linked to the previous block through a hashing mechanism. Each block contains the hash of the previous block's data, which creates the "chain" that holds them all together.

A hash is the fixed-length output from an algorithm called a hash function. Hash functions take inputs of different lengths and return a hash. When a new block is created on the blockchain, it receives a hash that includes a timestamp, information from the previous block, and the new block's transaction data.

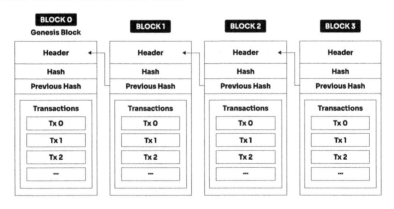

The structure of a block in blockchain

Whether you input the letter "A," the script for Shakespeare's Hamlet, or every line of dialogue in a Monty Python movie, a hash function will always return a hash of the same length. Hash algorithms are one-way functions: you can input Hamlet and receive its unique hash, but you can't look at the hash and see any clues that it's pointing to Hamlet.

Think about hashes as fingerprints for data. Your fingerprint is a unique identifier for you. If the FBI gets ahold of your fingerprint, they can use it to point to your picture in a database. But if the FBI gets ahold of a picture of you, they can't use the picture to determine your fingerprint. It's a one-way system.

Nonce: A Nonce—not to be confused with the English curse word— is an abbreviation for "number only used once." Nonces are added to hashed or encrypted blocks in a blockchain. It is a 32-bit number generated randomly when a miner creates a new block. Each nonce is unique and random. Nonces and hashes are critical security features for the blockchain, acting as one of the world's most secure versions of a password.

The Blockchain Cycle

With a basic understanding of the blockchain's core components, we can see how they work together. Let's take a look at how blockchains grow from the first transaction to an ongoing cycle of secure data storage.

1. Genesis Block

All blockchains begin with a single block called the Genesis Block. This first block serves a unique function, which we can understand by studying Bitcoin's Genesis Block. (Which also happens to be the first ever Genesis Block—the Genesis Genesis Block, if you will.)

Bitcoin devotees still donate small amounts of their cryptocurrency to the Genesis Block, even though the money that moves in can never be moved out. They see it as a tribute to Nakamoto and the future of Bitcoin, tossing in a few satoshis like Disney fans toss quarters into Mickey-shaped fountains.

All blockchains have a Genesis Block, although most are less rousing than Bitcoin's. Genesis Blocks act like ancestors for all of their descendants, the blocks that follow on the chain. Every block added to the chain contains a reference to the one before, so even the Bitcoiin transactions from ten seconds ago trace back to Nakamoto's 2009 Genesis Block.

Once the Genesis Block is established, new transactions can take place on the blockchain. But the transactions aren't bundled up into blocks and added to the chain automatically. Each new group of information needs to be validated, and participants on the blockchain must also come to an agreement on how the information is added to the chain.

2. Validation & Consensus

Validation and consensus are two processes that often get confused with each other. Validation is the process of ensuring a blockchain transaction is legitimate. Blockchain validators, often called miners, use complex mathematical processes to verify blockchain transactions. Consensus methods require participants to determine and agree on the order of transactions on the blockchain. Let's look at an example to see how the validation and consensus processes take place on a blockchain.

Jill is in a group chat with her friends. She sends a message asking them if they want to meet up for drinks after work. Her friend Jane responds, "Yeah, let's meet at Buckets at 6 PM!"

But before Jane's message makes it to the chat, John also responds with, "Sure, how about The Taphouse at 7?"

Jimmy responds, "Sounds good!"

None of Jimmy's friends know whether he thinks Buckets at 6 PM or The Taphouse at 7 PM sounds good to him. Now the group has two different plans proposed, and they must reach a consensus on which plan they'll follow.

On the blockchain, new transactions are broadcasted to every node on the network like a text message is broadcasted to everyone in a group chat. Miners receive the broadcasts for a few different transactions and group them into a block. But not every miner receives the same transactions at the same time. Latency issues and other factors can create different combinations of transactions for miners, so each one ends up building their own block. Some miners might create the same block twice, and some blocks may include some combination of the same transactions.

Two miners on the Bitcoin blockchain, Bill and Steve, receive a handful of transactions as they're broadcasted. They each grab a few transactions and build their own blocks.

- Bill builds a block out of Transaction A, Transaction B, and Transaction C.

- Steve builds a block out of Transaction C, Transaction D, and Transaction E.

In exchange for their service to the blockchain, miners are rewarded for their efforts with a small amount of Bitcoin. Bill and Steve both want the reward, but they only get paid if their block is added. Who gets to add their block to the chain? Both of these blocks are built out of valid transactions. It might sound best to add both to the chain and give both miners their reward, but there's a slight problem with that plan... Transaction C.

Transaction C is a record of Jane paying Jill 1 BTC. (At the time of writing this, 1 BTC would be a lucrative transaction, but we're rolling with it for simple math.) If Bill and Steve both add their block to the chain, Jane will end up paying Jill 2 BTC (1 BTC twice!) Furthermore, if Jane's Bitcoin wallet only has 1 BTC in it, the second transaction would be invalid. Since we clearly can't let Bill and Steve both add their blocks, how do we decide which block is built and which is bumped off?

3. Consensus Mechanisms

Consensus Mechanisms allow miners to compete in a Blockchain Battle Royale. The winner is granted the honor of adding their block to the chain—and the extra Bitcoin for his trouble. The most common consensus method to date is the Proof-of-Work method:

In Proof-of-Work, Bill and Steve compete against each other to solve a cryptographic puzzle that will reveal the last block on the chain's nonce. The puzzle is solved through trial-and-error, and the odds of solving it are about 1 in 5.9 trillion. The nonce makes the transactions inside the blocks more secure—if a hacker spent every waking moment of their life trying to guess one single nonce on a blockchain, they'd never make it. Neither would their children. Or their grandchildren. Or their great-grandchildren.

Miners therefore rely on powerful computers to shuffle through solutions as quickly as possible. Whichever node—Bill's or Steve's—solves the puzzle first wins the spot on the blockchain. This method requires miners to have powerful, expensive equipment that pulls massive amounts of energy. Miners compete with each other through the puzzles, but they also compete to have the largest amount of energy to finish the puzzles the fastest. This competition can force Bill and Steve to upgrade from a Chromebook to a chrome-filled home office, and when every other miner on the chain makes similar upgrades, the cost (for the miners and the environment) grows out of control quickly.

In Proof-of-Stake, a newer and more energy-efficient consensus method, Bill and Steve each "stake" their odds of winning the block by putting their own tokens in a "jar." A token is randomly selected by a protocol, and whoever owns the token is chosen to validate and add their block.

Each miner can place as many tokens into the jar as he wants. If Bill throws in five tokens and Steve throws in one, Bill is more likely to be chosen. But if Bill's token is chosen and his block turns out to be invalid, he loses some of his tokens as a penalty. This method is more energy-efficient, but it creates an issue with miners hoarding cryptocurrency. The more they validate the more cryptocurrency they earn, and the more they earn the more they can validate.

Other consensus methods have popped up in new blockchains to try to solve some of the negative effects of Proof-of-Work and Proof-of-Stake.

- Proof-of-Capacity is a consensus mechanism that allows nodes on the blockchain network to share memory space with others to mine available cryptocurrency.

- Proof-of-Burn requires transactors to send small amounts of their tokens to inaccessible wallets.

- Proof-of-Activity combines PoW and PoS systems; the mining process works the same as PoW, but once a block is successfully validated, the PoS method chooses which miner's block is added to the chain.

There are hundreds of consensus mechanisms out there today. Some companies are building solutions for consensus mechanisms that remove the need for miners (and their cut of the transaction costs). Steem, a blockchain-based company with a platform to encourage artists to receive compensation for their work, introduced the Proof-of-Brain consensus method. Proof-of-Brain rewards blockchain users directly for their likes and comments within Steem's token-based community system. The World Food Programme Building Blocks project aims to provide humanitarian aid around the world, and their consensus mechanism validates internally with employees who don't require additional rewards for their work.

The mission statement for Bitcoin is specific to decentralization in the world of finance, but its goal spread across the blockchain industry like wildfire. Blockchains aim to function in democratic environments, and consensus mechanisms are replacements for centralized agencies. When they work, they have the potential to be efficient, fair, real-time, reliable, and secure ways of performing transactions. Like all things blockchain, consensus mechanisms are still in their early stages. But as blockchain technology improves, so will the methods we use to validate it.

As more people, businesses, and industries adopt the technology, we will see how transformative blockchains will be. Blockchain's influence is mostly limited to the world of cryptocurrency right now, but there are some emerging blockchains stepping into the spotlight. These applications are only the beginning...the blockchain is going to transform every aspect of our lives. From storing college degrees to purchasing an apple, we're going to see how the blockchain will eventually be the foundation of everything we do.

CHAPTER 6

The Business of Blockchain

When we're young, we learn how some of our food can bite us back. We're taught to stay away from pink chicken, chunky milk, and tubs of raw cookie dough. Whether we learn from our parents, our friends, or a single unlucky experience, we know there are some foods out there that aren't worth eating, no matter how delicious they look. Sometimes, though, the same sour stomach can come from the food we learn to rely on for a healthy source of nutrition...and in 2018, a group of people learned this lesson the hard way from an unsuspecting source—a handful of leafy greens.

In the spring of 2018, 53 people showed up in hospitals across 16 different states for the same illness. The patients complained of severe abdominal cramping, nausea, vomiting, and varying degrees of diarrhea. Doctors recognized the symptoms of an E. coli infection and alerted the CDC. But until they could identify where the outbreak came from, the CDC couldn't issue a recall. They couldn't save others from suffering the same illness. It took two months of investigation to determine the culprit as a bad batch of romaine lettuce from a farm in Arizona. Without technology in place to track contaminated food from the farm to the patient's table, the investigation took far too long.

When an outbreak appears, a ticking clock counts down from the moment it's identified. Every moment without action results in another infection. As the CDC investigated the E. coli outbreak in 2018, the number of hospitalized people grew from 53 to 210. Five patients experienced kidney failure, but the agency still couldn't determine a common farm or distributor to issue a true recall. Every day that the CDC hit a dead end, more people poured through hospital doors. They needed to find the farm responsible, or people would die from infection.

Getting desperate, the agency resorted to interviewing patients from their hospital bed. Forty-one of the forty-three people they interviewed had eaten chopped romaine lettuce in a salad in the week before they fell sick. In a panic, the CDC released a statement telling everyone to stop buying and throw out any romaine lettuce, even if no one at home was sick yet.[19]

It wasn't until they interviewed patients from an Alaskan correctional facility that they found a general source for the outbreak. Yuma, Arizona was the only region to supply that particular correctional facility with chopped romaine lettuce. The CDC made phone calls out to all farms in Yuma, asking farmers to check their supply. But the CDC's efforts were too little, too late.

By the time they reached Yuma farmers, the season was finished and most lettuce had already been shipped out. The CDC moved to the production plants, but they collect and process lettuce from multiple ranches, making it impossible to isolate a single source. Worse, since lettuce only has a twenty-one day shelf-life, most plants had already shipped out their supply. The infected lettuce was in the supply chain.

The CDC's common traceback efforts are dangerously inefficient, as the 2018 outbreak revealed. Each step in their process takes an average of seven days to accomplish. To narrow down the source of an outbreak to a single farm is a several week process, and the total costs of the

---

[19] Center for Food Safety and Applied Nutrition. "Outbreak of E. Coli O157:H7 Infections Linked to Chopped Romaine Lettuce Grown in Yuma Region." U.S. Food and Drug Administration. FDA. Accessed June 7, 2022. https://www.fda.gov/food/outbreaks-foodborne-illness/fda-investigated-multistate-outbreak-e-coli-o157h7-infections-linked-romaine-lettuce-yuma-growing.

process were almost insurmountable. The outbreak wasn't officially announced to be "over" until three months after the initial illness appeared. Patients suffered from life-threatening symptoms, and some sustained permanent damage to their health.

Businesses along the supply chain for the contaminated romaine lettuce were shocked at how slow their tracking systems proved to be. Grocery stores lost millions when they cleared entire sections of their shelves. A new system was needed. One company in particular decided to make an effort to improve their systems: Walmart.

Walmart and Sam's Club signed up for a new system, IBM's Food Trust, that used blockchain technology to trace products. The blockchain allowed transparency for their products from farm to table. Now, when an outbreak appears from contaminated leafy greens, its barcode contains every piece of identifying information the CDC needs: what farm it came from, where it was processed, when it was shipped, and how long it's been on the shelf. Steps that used to take seven days with a paper ledger now took about 2.2 seconds. When the next outbreak occurred in fall 2018, the CDC knew the source and issued a recall after only four days.[20]

The CDC isn't the only agency that can benefit from blockchain's technology. Businesses that apply blockchain solutions can see more efficiency, transparency, and traceability across the board. Not every solution will determine life-or-death improvements, but companies can make groundbreaking innovations to the way they do business around the world.

We're going to take a look at the top five industries poised to see revolutionary benefits from blockchain technology. We'll catch a glimpse of how blockchains are being used already. Then, we'll explore

---

20   Tyko, Kelly. "Walmart Recall: Tanimura & Antle Romaine Lettuce
      Recalled from More Than 1,000 Walmart Stores Over E. Coli Risk."
      USA Today. Gannett Satellite Information Network, November 10,
      2020. https://www.usatoday.com/story/money/shopping/2020/11/10/
      walmart-recall-2020-romaine-lettuce-tanimura-antle-ecoli-contamination/6233817002/.

the precedent the new technology sets and examine how it might be improved and expanded in the future.

1. Banking

The blockchain is making its way into the banking world. As of 2018, 91 percent of banks had already invested in blockchain solutions.[21] Despite the fact that blockchain technology is one of the biggest threats to the banking sector, big banks like Goldman Sachs, J.P. Morgan, and HSBC are hoping to get into blockchain before it disrupts the industry without them.[22] In November, 2021, the Federal Reserve System in the U.S. released a joint statement about blockchain technology that officially recognized the emergence of cryptocurrency and **cryptoassets** (digital assets that use cryptography to regulate their value).[23] The Board of Governors promised to evaluate ways to integrate blockchain-based valuables into traditional banking practices.

Banks using blockchain-created processes that allow transactions outside of the Federal Reserve's banking hours to speed up approval time for payments. By coupling these transactions with smart contracts, costs for international payments have reduced for smaller banks and their clients. When every bank teller in the approval process is replaced by a smart contract, transaction times decrease exponentially. User errors are reduced. Human security weaknesses are covered. From loan closings to invoices to fraud warnings, banks are improving their processes with the blockchain.

---

[21] "Blockchain for Financial Services." IBM. Accessed June 7, 2022. https://www.ibm.com/blockchain/industries/financial-services.

[22] Mulders, Michiel. "Which Major Banks Have Adopted or Are Adopting the Blockchain?" Blockchain Works. Blockchain Works, June 7, 2022. https://blockchain.works-hub.com/learn/Which-Major-Banks-Have-Adopted-or-Are-Adopting-the-Blockchain-.

[23] Board of Governors of the Federal Reserve System. "Joint Statement on Crypto-Asset Policy Sprint Initiative and Next Steps." FDIC, November 23, 2021. https://www.fdic.gov/news/press-releases/2021/.

In the current system, when we look at our balance in our bank accounts, we're not looking at the actual amount of money in the account. There is no bank vault with our name on it holding stacks of cash for us. Instead, we see a representation of how much money we've stored with our bank. Most banks take the majority of our money and loan it out, hoping we won't need to make any big withdrawals before they make a profit off of our earnings. However, when blockchain technology is used to keep track of our accounts, we customers will have an accurate and secure record of what banks do with our money. We could use the data to demand a bigger chunk of the returns our money provides to the banks. We could even decline to allow banks to invest our money.

With blockchain-based banking, the future of loans and credit also looks different. Blockchain-enabled lending provides a cheaper, more efficient, and more secure system for personal loans.[24] P2P loans can be approved among peers based on anonymous records of previous payments instead of credit reports or home ownership status. Users can borrow against digital assets instead of their house or car. Predatory credit systems will crumble under fairer, more secure systems. And that's just the beginning of blockchain-based revolutions.

2. Supply Chain Management

IBM's Food Trust blockchain had a breakout success with Walmart's recall capability, and it continues to have an impact on supply chain management. Food Trust is a network that connects participants across food supply chains through permissioned blockchains. Companies that use Food Trust can minimize food waste, improve sustainability and efficiency, and improve their food safety standards across the board.

In our current system, one third of all food produced globally is lost or wasted, totalling at about $35 billion a year.[25] A large percentage of this

---

[24] CB Insights. "How Blockchain Could Disrupt Banking." CB Insights Research. CB Insights, July 1, 2021. https://www.cbinsights.com/research/blockchain-disrupting-banking/.

[25] "The Cost of Food Spoilage: Cargo Data Corp." Cargo Data, June 13, 2018. https://cargodatacorp.com/cost-food-spoilage/.

waste comes directly from consumers who are unsure about the quality of the food in their fridge. Funky-smelling chicken, soft asparagus, and browning avocados seem safer in the trash than in our stomachs. After all, we know how long we've had it, but how long was it sitting on a shelf before we put it in our shopping cart? The expiration date gives a definite endpoint, but what if our food seems off three days before the date on the package? How do we know it's still safe?

IBM's blockchain solution stores digital records in a decentralized system accessible to all participants. This transparency can provide businesses with specific insight into where food waste occurs most within their supply chain. Then, they can make adjustments and track improvement in real time. A bad batch of lettuce will catch the distributor's attention before it hits the shelves, saving customers from potential harm. If a consumer isn't confident that their salmon is supposed to smell so fishy, they can scan its barcode and see how it was handled every step of the way, from farm to final sale.

Blockchain technology can improve supply chain management everywhere with improved traceability, security, and efficiency. If you order a package from a blockchain-based company, you'll not only receive an estimated delivery day—you'll receive an estimated delivery *hour*. A smart contract can issue a discount or refund if your package isn't handed off in time. If it never appears on your doorstep, you can check the blockchain for a confirmation of your payment, where the package was last located, and which department signed off on its last movement. Blockchain's security features can prevent porch pirates from changing your package's status to hide their crimes. And if your package contains a glass vase and it arrives in a million pieces, the blockchain's records can reveal the package's quality as it moved down the supply chain. Returns, exchanges, and refunds will be easier because you, and the company you ordered from, have a record of where every transaction went wrong.

Businesses and consumers want their products to be as authentic as possible, and blockchain's transparency allows everyone the opportunity to check for quality. For businesses, blockchain technology can provide transparency that reduces fraud and counterfeiting. Whether a business sells diamonds, purses, or pharmaceuticals, it can better understand how their products are at risk of passing through gray markets or diminishing in quality as they progress through the supply chain.

Businesses can also use blockchain features to streamline their supply chain. Smart contracts can alert manufacturers to produce product based on immediate demand. For example, when the newest Nintendo Switch game is released, Target can put a one-year smart contract in place that sends an order to Nintendo for one hundred new copies of the game every time one hundred copies are sold. This way, Target spends less money on inventory and Nintendo spends less on manufacturing by only replacing their supply based on their demand.

3. Healthcare

The coronavirus pandemic in 2020 revealed the importance of fast, accurate, and readily available medical information. One company, Aetsoft, designed a Digital Health Passport (DHP) so that patients and doctors have direct, easy access to medical records. With the DHP, patients can create a digital profile to store all of their medical data. They can add test results to the profile, and with a single QR code, they can share a secure view of their medical profile to authorized people.

The DHP utilizes all the best features of blockchain technology. DHP profiles are divided into sections, so not every authorized person receives access to the patient's entire profile. (There's no need to show the dentist any OB/GYN records.) Blockchain's instant verification methods add results from blood work, disease tests, and routine check ups as soon as they're available. While most people still call around to multiple doctor's offices to consolidate their medical profile, DHP users have a complete picture of their health profile available any time, anywhere, as long as they have Internet access.

DHPs give users access and control over their personal health data. Aetsoft designed the platform with cryptographic signatures to ensure users could share health data with approved parties in a secure, verifiable, and trusted way.[26] With the help of the blockchain, users had easy access to their medical information and could feel safe knowing their data was secure from anyone they didn't want to give access to.

If we continue to improve and expand this technology, we could transform the way healthcare functions today. Imagine visiting a new doctor's office and, instead of filling out a half-hour's worth of new patient paperwork, you show the nurse a QR code to scan. Now the office has all your previous medical history, signed, sealed, and delivered via the blockchain.

When you see the doctor, she sends your prescription straight to the pharmacy through the blockchain and the same QR code will allow you to pick it up. When any test results come through, you'll have access to them as soon as your doctor does. A smart contract will notify your insurance company when you meet your annual deductible. Your medical information will remain secure, but you'll have more control over what happens with it than ever before.

4. Government

It's no secret that government services tend to be one of the most grueling processes in our lives. Voting lines last for hours. Receiving a passport can take months and require a mountain of paperwork. Most of us would rather stop driving altogether than sit at the DMV for three hours just to be told we're missing a piece of paperwork. Thankfully, blockchain technology can provide solutions for all of these problems.

In the Baltic country of Estonia, the government decided to update their torturous processes and provide citizens with a solution: e-Estonia. A blockchain-based application, e-Estonia provides Estonians with access

---

[26] "Digital Health Passport." Aetsoft. Accessed July 11, 2022. https://aetsoft.net/products/digital-health-passport/.

to all of their information securely and efficiently.[27] Today, Estonians can place votes, pay parking tickets, and update their ID photos from home. Their systems include medical records (for the people and their pets) which allows them to take charge of their health. Estonians don't have to file their taxes or apply for a loan, because with one click they can share all the necessary information with the right authority. In fact, the only time an Estonian citizen must show up at a government building is to buy a house or express their will to get married.

The more governments adopt programs that allow their citizens to control their information via blockchain, the more united our world can become. Estonia now functions as a "borderless country," which allows logged-in foreigners to use some Estonian services as if they live in the country. Estonia encourages companies to base their virtual operations there—Skype got its start on virtual Estonian soil. If other countries adopted similar governing policies, concerns about immigration, democratic process interference, and even identity theft would practically disappear.

5. Cybersecurity

For all of the industries listed above to thrive on blockchain technology, strong cybersecurity processes are a must. The blockchain's encryption and decentralization keeps the information it stores safe from hackers and false information. Blockchain's security features are lightyears safer than even the strongest cybersecurity systems in use today, and as the industries that store our most precious data take advantage, our information becomes safer still.

Cybersecurity can feel like an existential problem to many people and businesses. When Equifax was hacked in 2017, millions of people felt helpless knowing their private information was leaked. In 2020, Google revealed they were also the victims of the largest attack of its kind in

---

[27] Heller, Nathan. "Estonia, the Digital Republic." The New Yorker, December 11, 2017. https://www.newyorker.com/magazine/2017/12/18/estonia-the-digital-republic.

history (a distributed denial-of-service, or DDOS attack). The attack broke the record previously set eight months before, when Amazon Web Services (AWS) was hit.[28] That record has been broken multiple times in the past two years. Many DDOS attacks use decentralized bots to send in false requests that flood a network with a virus.

Since decentralized attacks (like DDOS) aren't coming from a single source, they're almost impossible to stop. However, when a decentralized attack targets a decentralized system, it is much less effective. One node catching the virus doesn't shut down the whole network. Instead, it traps the virus within the node and makes it easier for blockchain participants to catch it. By decentralizing assets, companies secure their public, permissioned, or private networks as well as the data inside them.

Some companies that operate in the previously listed industries are demonstrating the benefits of blockchain's cybersecurity strength. Founders Bank, a company striving to become the world's first decentralized bank, uses decentralized storage methods, a public ledger system, and encryption methods to make sure its customers' transactions are secure. Philips Healthcare is a research firm that combines blockchain technology with Artificial Intelligence (AI) to analyze their healthcare system, recognize vulnerabilities, and secure large amounts of data. Australia's government partnered with IBM to implement a blockchain for storing sensitive government documents.[29] Each use case depends on blockchain's cybersecurity features to protect their data from hackers, scammers, and other malicious attackers.

When companies choose to use blockchain technology for security, transparency, and trustless transacting, their entire businesses can transform. Processes can streamline. Profits can soar. Customers can

---

[28] Napoli, Robert. "Council Post: How Blockchain Could Revolutionize Cybersecurity." Forbes. Forbes Magazine, March 7, 2022. https://www.forbes.com/sites/forbestechcouncil/2022/03/04/how-blockchain-could-revolutionize-cybersecurity/.

[29] Daley, Sam. "Wallets, Hospitals and the Chinese Military: 18 Examples of Blockchain Cybersecurity at Work." Built In, April 15, 2022. https://builtin.com/blockchain/blockchain-cybersecurity-uses.

trust. Businesses will harness a new mode of collaboration that will drive growth at levels we haven't seen since the introduction of the Internet.

Blockchain benefits don't end at the business level. Improvements to network security and process efficiency are promising, but blockchain technology can revitalize industries in ways that affect the average person's daily life. As more institutions integrate blockchain into their infrastructures, basic everyday actions will evolve for the better.

CHAPTER 7

Blockchain in Everyday Life

Blockchain technology might be permeating conversations by the water cooler, tech blogs, and Reddit forums, but where else is it headed? As blockchain becomes increasingly popular, its influence reaches some surprising places...like a Facebook group dedicated to raising chickens.[30]

The Backyard Chickens Facebook group, established in 2017, had about 90,000 members from all over the world. In this group, chicken homesteaders shared stories, concerns, and questions about their personal flocks of chickens. This little Backyard Chickens Facebook community brought fowl fanatics together to talk about the simple joys of chicken-rearing. The page was an escape from the more stressful parts of life, even for chickenless people who wanted a place to appreciate the lifestyle. But in October 2021, the members of Backyard Chickens were reminded of how pervasive emerging technology can be, even for those who want nothing to do with it.

One morning in October, Backyard Chicken members logged into their Facebook accounts to the sight of this message from the page's administrator, Connor Bradley:

> *Good afternoon.*

We know all good things must come to an end. Sadly, this group is no longer for chickens. Don't worry, tons of backyard chicken groups have been made. Did not want to leave y'all hanging, so please join those. However, if you're interested in crypto and maybe want to learn, you're free to stay.

Until then, God bless.

Before the Backyard Chicken community could figure out what to make of this strange message, the group's name changed from "Backyard Chickens" to "Crypto with Connor." Members kept trying to post about their chickens hoping the change was a joke, but none of their posts were approved. The only posts making it past the administrators were from Connor himself, and they were all about cryptocurrency. If users were deemed too pushy about their poultry posts, they were blocked from the page altogether. Without any explanation, the chicken community focused on Connor.

Connor tried to be graceful with his group's transition, but the members were furious with him. They left nasty comments on his crypto posts. A few users even tracked down his mother's business and left bad Google reviews.

"These chicken people are crazy," Connor said, "You wouldn't believe how mean chicken people can be when something doesn't go their way."

Connor's motivations for changing the group were pure—he learned about cryptocurrency just in time to cash in on Dogecoin before it tanked. He knew he had an audience of 90,000 people on Facebook, and while they mostly talked about the best ways to cure bumblefoot (a common bacterial infection in chickens), Connor truly believed he could help them earn some money.

Although Connor's methods may not have been the best for garnering interest or excitement about cryptocurrency, he recognized the promise in it. He wanted to bring in as many people as possible to share it with them. Unfortunately, his approach isolated an entire community, and unnecessarily so! Cryptocurrency may have been the first application of blockchain technology, but crypto is just one piece of the puzzle. With all of the possible new applications emerging, even chicken farmers can find a few interesting applications for blockchain technology.

For example, if Connor introduced his Backyard Chickens page to Chikn[31], he might have caught their attention a little better. With Chikn, virtual farmers can purchase digital chickens (NFTs) and raise them in a Roost (digital wallet). The more the farmers tend to their chicks, the more $eggs (a type of cryptocurrency) those chickens lay. It's a world designed to be the virtual equivalent of chicken farming, except in this landscape, some chickens are made of lava and none of them catch a case of bumblefoot.

Crypto, NFTs, and other new blockchain ventures aren't going away any time soon. As we explore all the new ways blockchain technology can make our lives richer, safer, and more efficient, we can expect to discover it in some unusual places. Blockchain applications for almost every interest already exist. Whether we're real estate agents, car salespeople, or chicken farmers, we're going to see the effects of new blockchain applications everywhere.

The specific aspect of blockchain technology that has the potential to transform every aspect of society is called **tokenization.** Blockchain **tokens** are digital representations of assets (virtual or physical) and they are tied to the value of the asset. Tokenization is the process of transforming ownership rights into one or more digital tokens.[32] The applications for tokenization are only limited by the stretch of our imagination.

That being said, it would be impossible to cover every possible application for blockchains and tokenization. So, we're going to focus

---

[31] "Chikn." chikn. Accessed June 9, 2022. https://chikn.farm/.

[32] "Everything You Need to Know about Tokenization." 101 Blockchains, May 5, 2022. https://101blockchains.com/tokenization-blockchain/.

on four massive categories where blockchain technology is likely to change the way society functions. Within each application, we'll examine use cases already in place, precedents already set, and future implications we can look forward to seeing.

The Future is Paperless

Have you ever been on your way to the airport and suddenly realized you left your passport sitting on the counter? What about your boarding pass? Have you ever had your passport damaged, destroyed, or stolen? What about your driver's license? Or your work ID badge?

It can be frustrating to rely on all sorts of physical documentation just to prove your identity. The World Economic Forum, an organization that stretches across multiple countries, came up with a solution to this issue. They built a program called the Known Travel Digital Identity (KTDI) to promote secure, seamless travel without the need for physical paperwork to prove identity.[33] Travelers' personal information, usually divided between a driver's license, passport, and boarding pass, are all tokenized and stored in a cryptographically secure digital wallet. Through the blockchain, KTDI enables people to self-manage their identities from any mobile device.

While the KTDI program is still in its pilot stage, we can follow its implications to other industries that require paperwork to participate in. In the future, digital wallets could store our college transcripts, diplomas, and certifications. They may also store our licenses to drive, fish, hunt, boat, fly, and raise agricultural animals (like chickens). We could even store ownership information like the deeds to our homes, vehicle titles and registrations, and receipts for small purchases.

Digital wallets can store all the information we need to declare ourselves, but that doesn't mean everyone who asks gets an all-access pass to

---

[33] "KTDI Frequently Asked Questions." Known Traveler Digital Identity. World Economic Forum. Accessed June 9, 2022. https://ktdi.org/.

our personal data. The technology allows users to grant, restrict, and share access to their data with whoever, wherever, whenever. If a hiring manager asks to see a college transcript, we can choose to give access to it without letting them see our less impressive high school transcript. Airport security needs to see your passport data, but that doesn't mean they can see you are licensed to harvest oysters for the 2022 season. Part of the blockchain's beauty lies in its ability to give us control over our own information, whether it's on paper or not.

No more checking three times for your passport before you leave the house for vacation. No more fumbling through the glove box to present your license and registration. No more "two forms of ID" for painful verification processes. You can pull up tokenized versions of whatever ID information you need with the push of a button—including your signature—thanks to the blockchain.

We can think of these digital wallets as a set of lockers we're carrying around in our pockets. Each locker contains a document—or a set of documents—and we can give out the keys (our public keys) based on which documents an organization needs. Once they've seen the document and verified it, we can take the keys back, and they won't have access again unless we give them a new key. Our public keys point to our wallets, and the combination of our public and private keys serve as our own digital signature. This is handy, because very soon paper contracts will also be ditched for blockchain technology.

Current contract creation processes take too long, rely on large legal teams, and involve endless amounts of printed paper. Contracts on the blockchain are more secure, visible, and efficient. Blockchains make it so each party has a secure view of their shared contract. Any revisions require approval from every member, and all changes are captured on the blockchain. Contract drafts, rule-based agreements, digital signatures, and automatic remittance can all be accomplished directly from the blockchain. Once the contract is agreed on by everyone involved, it is stored in a "vault" that can't be altered.[34] No third party needed, not even a notary.

The only real downside for this technology applies to anyone still under legal drinking, smoking, and gambling age. Sorry folks, but fake IDs are going to be a thing of the past.

Throw Away the Key

Digital wallets can function like a set of lockers, but they can also function like a set of keys. Technology for securing access to private possessions is all over the place. Modern cars have codes to unlock doors. Some homes use combination locks instead of deadbolts. Phones, computers, and tablets have passcodes to let us in. Digital codes have been replacing physical keys for decades now, but they aren't always more secure. But once we replace weaker, numerical key codes with cryptographically signed digital keys, the whole system will be more secure. And with extra security, we can explore what other assets can be virtually unlocked.

Digital keys have plenty of advantages over traditional keys. We can't lose our car keys if we store them digitally. We won't short out our hotel room keys by sticking them near our phones if the keys are *on* our phones. If we want to give a trusted friend or family member access to our house, we can do it without directing them to the obviously fake, hollow Hide-A-Key rock on our front steps.

Physical locks can be picked, and smart locks without blockchain backing can be hacked. Centralized smart locks send signals back and forth between digital locks and digital keys, and their journey from source to destination leaves them vulnerable to hackers hiding behind virtual trees in the digital dark. Let's say you're at a water park and you need to rent a locker to store your belongings. If the locker is hooked

---

34 "Blockchain Technology for Digital Contracting." Accenture. Accessed June 9, 2022. https://www.accenture.com/us-en/case-studies/about/ blockchain-contracts-harnessing-new-technology.

up to the Internet, it will receive a signal to lock or unlock from an app on your phone. But if a hacker intercepts the signal, they control the lock. They can lock you out or let themselves in as soon as you head for your first waterslide.

As a decentralized network, the blockchain is resilient to hackers looking to snag access to a smart lock or a digital key. Smart locks on blockchains use **Public Key Infrastructure (PKI)** to read smart contracts and secure transactions instead of sending or receiving signals. The locker will unlock when the terms of its smart contract are fulfilled—when you've paid. The locker is now registered under your private key, and no one else can open it. If you want to expand your rental, you can pay-as-you-go. The hacker won't be able to crack the locker's encryption, and if they try to brute-force the lock, the locker can notify security.

PKI technology is already emerging in the real world. A company in Switzerland is using blockchain technology to launch a smart-cycling rental program called smartmo.[35] Bicyclists can use smartmo to reserve bike parking spots, lock their bikes in a single-bike stall, and charge e-bikes securely by using their private key.

If we combine digital keys with our personal identification, the possibilities grow even further. We can make hotel reservations and receive our room key through the blockchain. We can rent vacation homes, hotel rooms, and cars by using digital keys, and when our time is up the key expires without us dropping anything down a return slot. The QR codes that represent our wallets can be scanned to give us entry to concerts, movies, and other events. We can verify our identities and receive our digital keys all from one convenient location.

Digital keys not only have the potential to make our lives more convenient—they can make everything in our lives more secure. The whole point of keys is to protect access to our most valuable possessions.

---

[35] CoreLedger. "How Blockchain Makes a Smart Lock Even Smarter." Medium. CoreLedger, September 25, 2019. https://medium.com/coreledger/how-blockchain-makes-a-smart-lock-even-smarter-520d01176f4b.

With the security features the blockchain offers, we can use digital keys to make our protection efforts even safer.

Share the Wealth

Although cryptocurrency is the most popular way to invest using blockchain technology, tokenization of physical assets has the potential to transform the way we invest. When a physical asset is tokenized, its value is divided among those tokens. Each token represents a portion of ownership, and when the tokens are divided among different owners, they function as shares.

Tokenization that divides ownership of an asset across multiple owners introduced a new, democratic investment strategy. While an empty office building might cost $10 million—limiting ownership access to giant corporations, institutional investors, and government bodies— that value could be split into pieces through tokenization. The building could be worth 100,000 tokens valued at $100 each, and investors across the globe could buy and trade them. Smart contracts and secure ledger technology would ensure each investor receives their share of the income that building generates in the future.

Democratizing investments like real estate, luxury goods, and artwork removes a barrier of entry for the average worker.[36] A blue-collar employee probably can't invest in a $10 million building. Even if she could put down a hefty down payment, it's unlikely that an organization would approve such a high loan amount. However, she could probably afford to buy a token or two to generate some passive income. As her investments grow, she can repeat the cycle with more tokens to increase her shares.

The same concept could apply to any asset commonly shared in today's world. Instead of renting an apartment, a group of four roommates

---

[36] Lu, Marcus, ed. "Blockchain Applications: Tokenization of Real Assets." Visual Capitalist, January 25, 2022. https://www.visualcapitalist.com/ blockchain-applications-tokenization-of-real-assets/.

could share an investment into a home by splitting up the tokens. If they live in the city, they can split the value of a car to save parking space. Instead of suffering the complicated (and expensive) process of selling when it's time to move on, they can list their tokens for sale to anyone, anywhere.

The blockchain makes it easier to invest and provides all the information a potential investor needs to inform their decision. For real estate investors, a transaction record provides information that could make or break the sale. Was the building foreclosed? How many times has it changed hands in the last five years? Did any previous owners leave a warning note about the property in the block? Records on the blockchain are unchangeable, so if you want to know whether a home is haunted by previous owners, you can find out from the blockchain's records.

Companies like CARFAX and Kelley Blue Book provide a car's history and estimated value, but they only give this information at a price. Blockchains could eliminate those middlemen for buyers. Before you buy a car, you can see a detailed description of who owned it, whether it has been in an accident, and the date of its last tune-up. The blockchain's ledger will inform any potential buyer whether their new car is one of luxury or if it's a lemon.

The Internet of Things

You've heard of street smarts, but what about Smart Streets?

Imagine walking to your car, scanning your private key, and hopping in the *back* seat. Your favorite music station automatically plays and the cabin temperature adjusts to a comfortable 72 degrees. While you respond to a few work emails, your car spends the trip coordinating silently with the hundreds of smart devices on the road. Sensors in your bumpers, stop lights, stop signs, the lines on the road, and available parking spots all direct your car along the safest route to your destination.

This is the height of luxury, you think as you scroll through Twitter.

Smart streets are only one example of how the Internet of Things industry will make everyday life move smoother. The **Internet of Things** (IoT) refers to the ever-growing network of connected devices that share, analyze, and act on data to optimize certain conditions.[37] While some IoT critics might think it's overkill to own a smart toaster, the applications for this technology expand much further than a bluetooth toaster that knows your preferred level of toastiness.[38]

The Internet as we know it has connected people in life-changing ways. This next evolution will connect all of our devices and allow them to communicate similarly. This doesn't mean our air fryers are going to Tweet their hot takes about climate change, but it *does* mean our air fryers can communicate with other devices in our kitchen to make sure the food it's cooking will finish at the same time as the food on the stove.

Exciting applications for IoT technology are already in action. Some applications exist on a scale as small as smart homes. Simplisafe's home security package—complete with burglary sensors, indoor and outdoor cameras, panic buttons, and hazard sensors—has all of its devices in constant communication to determine threat levels and decide the best course of action without user input. Is there a fire or a thief? The system will use its sensors to decide, and it will alert the homeowners as well as the correct authorities.[39] Other industries expand IoT applications outside the comfort of our homes to our neighborhoods, whether we're living the rural life or residing in a big city.

---

[37] Thomas, Mike. "30 Internet of Things Examples You Should Know." BuiltIn, June 6, 2022. https://builtin.com/internet-things/iot-examples.

[38] Hruska, Joel. "The Internet of Things Has Officially Hit Peak Stupid." ExtremeTech, January 5, 2017. https://www.extremetech.com/electronics/242169-internet-things-officially-hit-peak-stupid-courtesy-smart-toaster-griffin-technology.

[39] "Wireless Home Security Alarm System: Simplisafe Features." Wireless Home Security Alarm System | SimpliSafe Features. Accessed June 9, 2022. https://simplisafe.com/meet-the-system.

Cities all over the world are using IoT tech to build smarter systems. In Tel Aviv, Israel, a company called Optibus analyzes data to plan and schedule bus routes around real-time road congestion. In Cambridge, U.K., Telensa uses IoT sensors for smart street lighting. In Chicago, ParkWhiz helps people find and price off-street parking for immediate or future trips into the city.[40] There are dozens of companies working to build platforms for smart intersections, smart parking, and smart roadways. The more cities' devices can communicate with each other, the safer, smarter, and more efficient cities become.

Add blockchain technology to IoT, and all the data those devices send and receive becomes much safer. If smart cameras collect 24-hour video to monitor traffic patterns, storing the footage on the blockchain prevents any agency or individual from altering it. It also prevents anyone from removing it or restricting access to it. Remember that the blockchain is designed to democratize our data, not sell every bit of information to the highest bidder.

IoT applications built on a blockchain foundation ensure we don't end up in an Orwellian nightmare where Big Brother keeps his eye on us through a sensor on a smart scooter. This speculation does bring up a valid concern, though. How do we make sure our precious data doesn't fall into the wrong hands? How do we know all the data stored on blockchains is safe? How can we trust one system to keep our ID information, our medical history, our certifications and licenses, and our money safe from hackers and outages?

If we're going to store our entire identity in a single storage space, we'd better be sure it's more secure than a steel safe buried beneath six feet of cement.

---

40 Thomas, Mike. "9 Companies Helping Create the IoT Smart City." Built In. Accessed June 9, 2022. https://builtin.com/internet-things/iot-smart-city-applications.

CHAPTER 8

Blockchain Security

As new blockchain applications appear, so do new security vulnerabilities. Each new virtual building popping up on the blockchain's skyline has at least one backdoor for hackers to exploit. On April 30, 2016, a program called a Decentralized Autonomous Organization (DAO) launched on Ethereum's blockchain. A DAO is an organization with no centralized leadership, meaning it is member owned and governed by rules encoded as a transparent computer program. The Ethereum DAO had the intention of transforming the way people invest, but it ended up teaching blockchain pioneers a lesson in the risks associated with the emerging technology.[41]

The DAO quickly raised $150 million USD worth of ether (ETH), but less than three months after its launch, hackers broke into the program and stole $70 million in ETH from investors. Ethereum wanted to return the stolen funds, but to do so was to act in conflict with what makes blockchain so attractive. If Ethereum wanted to recover the stolen funds, they would have to *change* their blockchain. Their chosen course of action is now an infamous example of blockchain security concerns.

---

[41] Cryptopedia Staff. "The Dao: What Was the DAO Hack?" Gemini. Cryptopedia, March 16, 2022. https://www.gemini.com/cryptopedia/the-dao-hack-makerdao.

The Ethereum DAO (or decentralized autonomous organization) was the first of many firms designed to act as an investor-directed venture capital cooperative. DAOs open up an investment cycle during which the collected funds are locked up. (Picture the world's strongest bank vault surrounded by the world's beefiest security team.) When the cycle is finished, investors can vote on how they want to share the funds they've gathered.

Whether stakeholders want to invest their DAO pot in an empty office building, a Baskin Robbins franchise, or an auction bid for the United States Constitution (yes, this really happened), all investors must reach a consensus to spend the funds. The office building could become low-income housing or a 24-hour rave space. The Baskin Robbins franchise could feature a 32nd flavor called "Pineapple Upside-DAOwn Cake." If the investments don't work out, they can be returned, like the funds for the Constitution were when the DAO lost the auction. Whatever their purpose, all DAO rules, decisions, amendments, and actions must pass a vote from all stakeholders before they can take effect.

Without security and trust, DAOs would never function as a solid investment option for anyone. No investor would throw thousands of dollars into a sack and think, *I bet this group of strangers online will take good care of my money.* The strict governance of DAOs call for strong software, and blockchain technology's immutability, transparency, and visibility made it a perfect foundation for DAO structures. Instead of a firm taking control of investors' money, the code would manage the funds automatically and according to the votes. It seemed like the perfect solution, until hackers broke in and stole $70 million in ETH.

11,000 people invested in the DAO in its twenty-eight day investment window, but as they explored the details of their new venture, some noticed a few vulnerabilities in the DAO's code, especially in its smart contracts. The investors voiced their concerns because they wanted to see it fixed, but unfortunately a few hackers also heard their cries and attacked before Ethereum's engineers could patch the code. With only a few short days remaining in the investment period, the hackers began to drain the DAO's funds.

Ethereum's community debated how to respond to the unprecedented attack. Even though the attack was a result of the DAO's code and Ethereum itself worked perfectly, the Ethereum community still felt a responsibility to help resolve the problem for their own sake. The blockchain was less than a year old, and the DAO's failure would not only devastate investors, but the future of blockchain applications everywhere. 14 percent of all ETH was tied up in the DAO, and losing that volume of cryptocurrency to a single attack put Ethereum—and blockchain technology at large—on the brink of extinction.

Ethereum's initial response to the hack was the proposal of a **soft fork**, which is a software update that sets new rules for new blocks while still recognizing old, valid blocks. Soft forks create one-time fixes on the blockchain that seal a block and stop tokens from moving in or out. A soft fork of the Ethereum network involved adding code that would blacklist the hackers from moving or using their stolen funds. The hackers' tokens would be frozen in place, unable to move from their wallet ever again. It meant the investors would lose their stake, but at least the hackers wouldn't make a profit.

However, a hacker (or someone posing as a hacker) posted an open letter to Ethereum and claimed their tokens were obtained "legally" based on a loophole in the DAO's smart contract. Once their twenty-eight day waiting period was over, the tokens belonged to them. If Ethereum tried to seize the funds, the hacker promised to sue. Ethereum's community thought about calling the hacker's bluff...until they found a bug in the soft fork's update code that would open the blockchain up for another, possibly *bigger* attack.

Matters were made worse when the hacker threatened to bribe Ethereum miners to ignore a soft fork in exchange for a collective reward of one million ETH and 100 BTC. Ethereum's community wasn't sure how else to proceed with a solution that wouldn't jeopardize the moral expectations of the blockchain. They had to consider a more nuclear option. A hard fork.

A **hard fork** is an update that invalidates *all* previous blocks on the blockchain network. Ethereum knew a hard fork could solve their problem, but it broke one of the blockchain's cardinal features by changing the record.[42] Still, the twenty-eight day investment cycle was almost over, and once it ended the hacker would have full access to all of the stolen funds. Without a hard fork the DAO would be finished, and the hacker would win.

After several days of heated debate, the Ethereum community implemented the hard fork. The hard fork essentially rolled the blockchain back to the moment before the DAO attack and reallocated all the lost funds to a different smart contract investors could use to take them back. When the fork took place, the Ethereum team wiped their collective foreheads and breathed a sigh of relief...but not every user felt like the hard fork saved the day.

The fork split Ethereum's blockchain into two competing chains. Users who refused to recognize the hard fork stayed on the old blockchain, now called Ethereum Classic, or ETC. The blockchain commonly known as Ethereum today is the one with the hard fork.

This hack provided a wake-up call to blockchain developers by showing them the consequences of skipping the security checks in new blockchain platforms. If the blockchain is going to continue to set the standard for safe data storage solutions, users must be aware of the risks they face, now and in the future.

While the basic structure of the blockchain provides a data structure that has inherent security features, the applications built with blockchain foundations are more susceptible to attacks.[43] Blockchain backing

---

[42] Frankenfield, Jake. "Hard Fork (Blockchain) Definition." Investopedia. Investopedia, May 25, 2022. https://www.investopedia.com/terms/h/hard-fork.asp.

[43] "What Is Blockchain Security?" IBM. Accessed June 14, 2022. https://www.ibm.com/topics/blockchain-security.

doesn't make a network immune to cyber attacks or fraud, and there will always be bad apples that can worm their way into the smallest vulnerabilities in technology. Let's take a look at the most common ways a single bad hacker can spoil a whole blockchain.

Phishing Attacks

By now, most people with an email address have been the target of a phishing attempt. Thankfully, they're usually easy to spot. For example, if an email has the headline, "CONGRATULATIONS, YOU'VE WON!" but you haven't entered any contests that you can think of, it's probably a scam. And if Amazon wanted you to update your credit card number, they'd ask you on their website, not through an email from "aj3ufo2icn83e2@anazom.com." You never give your Social Security number to unverified sources, even if they're promising two tickets to an all-expenses paid cruise. And no one is ever trying to reach you about your car's extended warranty.

Unfortunately, phishing attempts aren't always so obvious. Scammers have evolved to use more creative methods. Since most blockchain users today are pretty tech-savvy, successful phishing attempts must be equally clever to steal private keys or passwords. In many ways, blockchain users are only beginning to understand how dangerous these attacks can be.

Take Gabby, for example, who when she bought her first set of NFTs had no idea how valuable her purchases would be, or that anyone would dream of stealing them from her.[44] Gabby was a Justin Bieber fan, and when he sponsored a line of teddy bear NFTs, she wanted in. She bought three mystery bears for about $900 USD each (in ETH) and thought she could keep one and sell the others to make her money back. But when she opened her wallet and "unwrapped" her new NFTs, she discovered she'd purchased one of the rarest bears in the collection.

---

[44] Anna Foley, Alex Goldman, and Emmanual Dzotsi, hosts, "The Rainbow Chain." Reply All (podcast), April 7, 2022, accessed June 14, 2022, https://gimletmedia.com/shows/reply-all/j4he7a7/185-the-rainbow-chain

Excited about her good fortune, Gabby posted about her bear in an inBetweeners chat on Discord. Other bear owners congratulated her in the public chat and private messages. In one of these private chats, an unfamiliar username sent her a message with a link. Gabby had heard of NFT projects sending free NFTs to people on Discord, so when the link asked her to verify her account she thought she'd gotten lucky for the second time that day. She was so thrilled to receive another bear that she didn't think twice about entering her public *and* private key into the link's form.

The link was a phishing scam. Moments after submitting her private information, all three of her bears disappeared from her digital wallet. Gabby watched in horror as her NFTs bounced around the market. At first they sold for $3,000 in ETH. Then they sold for $6,000. Then $12,000. But while she could observe the transactions of her stolen bears, she couldn't track down the person who stole them.

Gabby had no way to make her money back. There was no bank to contact about identity theft, and no administration behind the NFTs to catch the thief or return the bears. In mere moments, the NFTs had been traded away to another user, and then another, and then another. They were gone, all because of a simple phishing link.

Phishing attacks are the most common form of cyber attack, and they're not going anywhere. These attacks work so well because they occur on the user end of the technology—as opposed to the backend—and therefore cannot be patched with code. Phishing hackers rely on innocent users to let down their guards, using tempting bait to lure them into providing sensitive information. As blockchain applications evolve, so will phishing attempts, so users must stay vigilant and keep their private keys locked up tight.

Sybil Attacks & 51 Percent Attacks

In a 1973 nonfiction book by Flora Rheta Schriber, a little girl named Sybil has over fifteen personalities. Some are kind, like Mary Lucinda and The Blonde. Some are cruel, like Peggy Lou and Clara. And some are underdeveloped, like Ruthie the baby. Sybil's story is an in-depth look at some of the more confusing, overwhelming, and complicated aspects of DID, or Dissociative Identity Disorder (previously known as multiple personality disorder). Sybil is also the name given to a category of deceptive cyberattacks.

The Sybil attack is named after Sybil because it is carried out by hackers who create multiple identities within the same node. A Sybil attack on social media could involve making a dozen Twitter accounts to boost a Tweet's "like" count, file multiple complaints against an account the hacker dislikes, or to spam the hacker's favorite band with "SEND FREE TICKETS PLS" from twelve different usernames. On the blockchain, Sybil attacks are more dangerous because each false identity has more functionality.

Sybil hackers on the blockchain flood a network with false network identities to control as many nodes as possible.[45] Once the hacker controls multiple nodes, they can out-vote other honest nodes, block transmissions, or refuse to validate blocks, effectively stopping the network. In large-scale Sybil attacks, hackers can take over enough nodes on a network to carry out a 51 percent attack. This is when problems *really* begin for blockchains.

Since blockchains are democratic systems, each node has equal power, and any actions that take place have to be approved by the majority of the nodes on the network. 51 percent attacks destroy the democracy of the blockchain and transfer all of the power to a single user. If a hacker successfully takes over 51 percent of the nodes in a 51 percent attack, they gain control over the blockchain ledger and can manipulate it however they want. They can block transactions from being validated, reverse previously validated transactions, and even spend single tokens more than once.

---

[45] Binance Academy. "Sybil Attacks Explained." Binance Academy. Binance Academy, October 4, 2021. https://academy.binance.com/cs/articles/sybil-attacks-explained.

It stands to reason that bigger blockchain networks have a better defense against a 51 percent attack. Hacking three nodes in a five-node-network is substantially easier than hacking 2,054,691 out of the 4,109,380 nodes running on Ethereum's network. Bitcoin, Ethereum, and other gigantic blockchains are unlikely to suffer successful 51 percent attacks, but that doesn't mean they're completely immune. It's simply so difficult and expensive to collect the equipment and computing power needed to carry out an attack, any hackers capable of doing it would actually make more money as honest BTC miners!

Computer scientists are still working to build better protection against Sybil and 51 percent attacks, and their results have varying degrees of effectiveness. Consensus methods like PoW and PoS defend against Sybil attacks. PoW makes the amount of work each node completes on the network too complicated for a false identity to complete. PoS assigns work to nodes based on reputation, which makes it less likely that "new" (fake) nodes will have an opportunity to affect the blockchain.

Routing Attacks

Although blockchains have stronger defenses than other centralized applications on the Internet, any system that uses an internet connection can fall victim to a routing attack. Blockchains' nodes use the Internet to pass data back and forth. Routing attacks travel through Internet Service Providers (ISP) to affect participation in web-enabled systems.

Imagine the path the data takes from one node to the next as a highway. A routing attack puts up a giant barricade in the middle of the highway, causing the traveling data to stop in its tracks and either find a way around or wait for the blockage to clear. If the data stops and waits, the blockchain network slows to a halt. If the data goes around, it may fall right into a trap set up by the hacker on either side of the barricade. Now the hacker has control of that data. They can read its contents, delete it, or hold onto it. This stops the node that sent it from validating any more blocks on the chain.

In a routing attack, nodes and other blockchain participants are usually oblivious to the threat because other data transmissions and operations keep moving normally. It can take up to twenty minutes for anyone else to catch signs of an attack, but by then a hacker could have tampered with dozens of blocks. Since routing attacks can cause lasting damage behind the scenes, it's imperative that blockchain applications use secure routing protocols to make sure their data stays safe during travel.

Vulnerabilities & Other Security Concerns

Hackers are like virtual rats crawling through the narrowest virtual corridors—as long as they can find a hole big enough to stick their head through, they can wiggle into any program and exploit it for their own gain. Decentralized apps, DAOs, and other applications written on the foundation of the blockchain must secure their code to prevent security issues from affecting their users. Establishing a secure blockchain platform is imperative to avoiding hacks that can devastate new technology before it has a chance to take off.

Ethereum took a lot of the heat from the DAO attack, but the reality is their blockchain functioned perfectly. The vulnerabilities came from the DAO's software program and its smart contracts. The DAO's smart contract completed cryptocurrency transfers *before* it confirmed the amount remaining in the DAO wallet. This meant the hacker could request currency fast enough to secure the same ETH multiple times before the smart contract could update its balance.[46] This issue was labeled a recursive call, and it appeared as a loophole because the DAO's smart contract wasn't properly audited before it launched.

Blockchain operates on the foundation of consensus, decentralization, and cryptography to ensure trust and transparency for its users. However, no technology is completely hack-proof, especially not while

---

[46] Falkon, Samuel. "The Story of the DAO - Its History and Consequences." Medium. The Startup, August 12, 2018. https://medium.com/swlh/the-story-of-the-dao-its-history-and-consequences-71e6a8a551ee.

pioneers are exploring all of its possibilities. Although the security issues listed above are the most common attacks seen on the blockchain since its start, there are a couple other challenges worth keeping an eye on:

Endpoint Attacks: Endpoint attacks are aimed at places where users interact with the blockchain. Hackers may not be able to access the blockchain, but they can penetrate phones, laptops, tablets, and other electronic devices to monitor people's activities and steal private keys. The best ways users can protect themselves against endpoint attacks is by installing antivirus software, not storing private keys on personal devices, and reviewing the systems they use regularly.

Replay Attacks: Replay attacks happen after a blockchain uses a hard fork to split between legacy (the old blockchain) and new. The hacker then uses transactions that were validated on the legacy blockchain and replays them on the new one. If the hacker passed ten BTC from one wallet to another on the legacy blockchain, he can replay the transaction to keep moving ten BTC on the new blockchain. Miners will recognize the transaction details as valid and push them through, even though that value didn't exist on the new blockchain. Developers can preemptively stop replay attacks by adding code to the fork that guarantees transactions from the legacy blockchain won't be approved on the new one.

More Secure, not Totally Secure

My favorite definition of "security" came from a New York City bouncer:

"There's a reason the back of my jacket says 'security,' and not 'safety.' Nightlife isn't safe, and it's not my job to make it safe. That's not what security is. Security is going into unsafe environments and mitigating as many threats to safety as possible."

Let's not pretend the use of any technology is safe. There will always be hackers trying to take advantage of technological weaknesses. If we really want to be *safe*, we can turn off all our devices and never get on the internet again, but for most of us this is unrealistic. So, rather than hope for a world where security threats don't exist, we must acknowledge the risks and do our part to mitigate as many as possible.

Every time we use technology to help us manage our lives, we assume different levels of risk. The blockchain is no exception. All of the attacks covered here have been around for decades, but before the blockchain they worked to target Internet applications. Before the Internet, these "hacks" involved less coding and more grifting. A hacker could carry out a routing attack by intercepting a package while it travels on a literal highway. A phishing attack could steal Social Security numbers by asking for it in person or through a written letter in the mail. Security concerns are nothing new, all that changes are the ways hackers evolve to catch us and the ways we must evolve to avoid being caught.

One of the best ways to mitigate security threats is to be aware of what the threats are. When blockchain technology starts popping up in every corner of our lives, we'll be better prepared for possible security breaches because we'll know what to look for. We'll avoid phishing attacks, help spot sybil attacks, and point out other vulnerabilities to developers in ways that don't also alert hackers to the weak spots. The blockchain can bring an era of advanced data storage solutions to the entire world, but the technology will only be adopted when the majority of people feel it is as secure as the processes they've used their whole lives.

CHAPTER 9

Blockchain's Biggest Challenge

Nothing crushes potential like the unmet expectation of perfection. To see this in action, look no further than the institution of marriage. Do couples succeed because they expect their partner to be the perfect spouse? Of course not! If that were true, the divorce rate would skyrocket.

Marriages succeed because both partners know their love is *not* about perfection. Instead, their success comes from little wins every day that make the relationship worth continuing. Bad days, stressful fights, and hard moments don't lead the couple to abandon their relationship. The best marriages choose to focus on small wins—date nights, resolved fights, finishing a kitchen remodel. Little victories remind couples their relationships are worth growing and their problems are worth solving. They chose to marry because they share a promising foundation, and they choose to build from that despite the moments they feel like they're failing.

If people approached emerging technologies the way newlyweds approach their relationship, they'd be more likely to see the full benefits of the technologies after their early kinks are worked out. Too often, people dismiss emerging technologies because of unrealistic expectations for perfection. If an exciting new online game crashes, players can be unforgivingly furious, even though the studio may be experiencing unprecedented demand on their servers. And if self-driving cars are not *perfect*, manufacturers will be hard pressed to see their vehicles go farther than the factory line. (Never mind the fact that human drivers are far from perfect themselves!) To see new technologies succeed, people must understand these innovations need time to grow. It's not about, "How can we be perfect?" It's about, "how can we be better?"

The blockchain is an emerging technology facing the same types of growing pains as any new marriage. Many people may be reluctant to accept blockchain technology so long as it has obvious imperfections, but if the technology isn't given time to work out its early kinks, it may end up divorced from the general public. It's the public's job to recognize blockchain technology's strong foundation, and to encourage its growth by celebrating its little victories.

The Court of Public Opinion

The biggest threat to the blockchain's growth potential is the public's opinion. Media outlets publish the blockchain's biggest successes and failures. Since the blockchain is a large-scale, disruptive, interesting innovation, news sources love to focus on its developments—and not all of their articles show the technology in a flattering light.

It's not uncommon for media outlets to hyperfocus on new developments, whether they're about a new technology or a new celebrity couple. Whenever two A-list celebrities tie the knot, the media takes the news and whips fans into a frenzy. Tabloids were flooded with stories about Sarah Jessica Parker and Robert Downey Jr. when they married in 1983 and split in 1991. Brad Pitt and Angelina Jolie dominated news cycles from 2005 to their divorce in 2016. Even people who have no interest in Keeping up with the Kardashians knew about Kim and Kanye's biggest relationship beats. No corner of celebrity relationships are safe—not their victories, successes, or struggles. And with every new article, big name couples are subjected to the court of public opinion.

There are two clear public opinions about the blockchain—there are people who love it and people who hate it, and there isn't much room in between. At a Bitcoin convention in March 2022, celebrities like Serena Williams and Aaron Rodgers proclaimed they signed deals to receive their paychecks in Bitcoin instead of cold, hard cash. Meanwhile, investment tycoon Warren Buffett has publicly shared his disgust with cryptocurrency multiple times, calling it "rat poison squared."[47] Every time the price of Bitcoin rises, Williams and Rodgers call it "proof of concept." Every time it drops, Buffett says, "I told you so."

When the people stuck in the center of the debate see equal confidence from either side, they find it tough to know what to believe. Financial experts, athletes, actors, and even Instagram influencers all make different claims about the future of the blockchain. Though their expertise may vary, their voices influence the public's opinion. They're not the only voices that sway public discord, though.

Tech media loves to focus on the cryptocurrency market for the same reason tabloids love Prince Harry and Megan Markle: because of the drama. Although cryptocurrency is only one application for blockchain technology, sensationalist news articles tend to focus their criticism of the blockchain as a whole on crypto performance. Bitcoin news fills financial headlines, but blockchain applications in the food safety sector aren't as likely to generate clicks online. Compounding the bad press, big breakdowns in blockchain technology are better at grabbing attention than blockchain's successes. However, blockchain's bad press isn't entirely without merit. If blockchain's pioneers are going to earn a more positive public opinion, they will have to address the following problems.

Losing the Keys

"Honey, have you seen my keys?"

---

[47]   Rothberg, Ethan. "Bitcoin's Crashing - Here's Why Warren Buffett Has Hated It All Along." Yahoo! Finance. Yahoo!, June 14, 2022. https://finance.yahoo.com/news/bitcoins-crashing-heres-why-warren-220000034.html.

This sentence *must* be somewhere on a list of top causes for divorce. No matter how many key hooks, pegs, or bowls a family sets up in their home, one spouse will inevitably fail to put the keys in their designated place. Every time one spouse admits their mistake, the next five minutes to half an hour are spent ripping up couch cushions, digging through laundry baskets, and ducking under furniture for a glimpse of shining silver keyrings. If people are this bad at keeping track of their keys, how will anyone survive in a system without a spare set?

Ever since keys have been used to open locks, there have been backup plans for when the keys get lost. Locksmiths can make new keys. Car dealerships can replace lost car keys. Even digital keys like passwords can be recovered if lost or forgotten. But on the blockchain, the lack of a controlling entity stops any business or person from helping people recover lost private keys. Once the key is gone, it's gone.

Blockchain users don't get to make up their own private key, as they would with other online passwords. Private keys are long, randomly generated combinations of letters and numbers. This means they're difficult to copy, but they're also difficult to memorize. Try memorizing and then typing from memory this sample key below:

63S9K2W2GMJ2GBUQVPQQIC74GIRTIZU3EEXF52F17GQSKGJSF5QE

And that's one of the shorter ones!

On the blockchain, your wallet is only as secure as your private key. All it takes for someone to access your blockchain data is your private key. You can write it down, but you risk losing the paper. You can keep it on a flash drive, but you risk misplacing it. You can store it on your phone or computer, but you risk exposing it to a hacker. And if someone else gets ahold of your key, they have control over anything in your wallet. This problem only exacerbates as digital wallets expand from storing cryptocurrency to birth certificates and Social Security numbers.

Storing private keys in complex, secure systems may seem like an acceptable risk to the average user, but when the blockchain grows to accommodate the majority of society there will be people who struggle to secure their keys. Many in the elderly community already have trouble with Internet accessibility, susceptibility to cyber attacks, and their physical memory capacity (for the key *and* where they stored it). People with cognitive or physical limitations may not have the means to control their information alone and must trust another person (or people) to control their key.

Before it can grow to its full potential, blockchain technology must work for all people. Hypr is a company working on passwordless authentication. Their goal is to give users easy access to blockchain wallets, email addresses, and more. Their platform allows users to access accounts through **multi-factor authentication (MFA)**. Hypr uses a combination of biometric data scanned with smartphones (like fingerprints and Face ID scans), and physical assets (like QR codes and physical tokens) to prove a user's identity without a password.[48] And since the company itself operates on the blockchain, Hypr doesn't store users' information for verification. With Hypr, people that would otherwise struggle to keep track of their private key can still reap the benefits of the blockchain.

Speed & Efficiency

If blockchains are going to run beneath our modern technology like the veins run under our skin, their processing times must improve exponentially. Blood in the average human's body moves at about three feet-per-second.[49] If it moved any slower, we'd struggle to move as fast, think as fast, and heal as fast. Driving cars, playing sports, and intensive surgeries would all be out of the question. In marriage, spouses must leap into action when their partner says, "I'm hungry,"...or else. Speed

---

[48] O'Connell, Justin. "The Future of IOT: Blockchain Biometrics with HYPR." Bitcoinist.com, August 2, 2016. https://bitcoinist.com/future-iot-blockchain-hypr/.

[49] Albert Vein Institute. (2019, October 22). *Do you know how amazing your veins are?* Albert Vein Institute. Retrieved June 19, 2022, from https://www.albertvein.com/blog/2018/june/do-you-know-how-amazing-your-veins-are-/#:~:text=How%20Fast%20is%20Blood%20Pumped%20Through%20Your%20Body%3F,gallons%20of%20blood%20an%20hour!

matters, and if blockchain can't find a way to validate blocks faster, many people may find the technology useless.

Blockchains like the ones running Bitcoin and Ethereum can only validate so many blocks per minute. Bitcoin validates a new block every ten minutes, and while that's not too long to wait for a money transfer confirmation, it's too long for a doctor to wait for access to a patient's medical records. It's too long for cars to register a key when people need to drive to a hospital. And it's *way* too long for a self-driving car to receive a signal from a red light. Without faster validation, the blockchain won't be able to carry out its most exciting applications.

There are ways to speed up the validation process, but they come with security risks. If PoW validators take shortcuts to decrease the time to validate new blocks, the consensus mechanisms won't be as strict. Blocks will be weaker. Even with PoS validation, sacrificing processing time also means sacrificing security. That's why programmers are developing other consensus mechanisms for future blockchain use—ones that won't require time-consuming consensus processes, but are just as secure as the ones that came before. Some of the methods were covered in Chapter 4, like Proof-of-Consensus, Proof-of-Burn, and Proof-of-Brain. These are examples of newer, faster, and more efficient validation methods designed to grow blockchains at greater speeds.

New consensus methods will make the blockchain smoother and quicker, but these are not the only improvements over the more popular PoW. Some improvements are also designed to tackle an even bigger barrier to the blockchain's global integration: the eco footprint.

Environmental Impact

The energy currently needed to validate blockchains is too high for expansion. There isn't an exact number for the energy used, but an estimation can come from networks' hash rates and energy consumption from mining rigs. Bitcoin's blockchain network alone was estimated to use 26.72 Terawatt-hours of electricity in the 2020 calendar year—more than the Netherlands, Argentina, or the United Arab Emirates.[50] It would take the average American household 74.01 days to use the same amount of energy.

These blockchains aren't only demanding energy, they're also creating a carbon footprint bigger than a coal-mining, litter-happy Bigfoot could make in a lifetime. The Bitcoin network is estimated to be responsible for 114 million tons of carbon dioxide per year, which is equal to the amount generated by the Czech Republic.[51] Ethereum generates about 48.69 million, the same amount generated by Bulgaria.

Most of the blockchain's energy consumption comes from mining cryptocurrency. The intensity of mining cryptocurrency was designed to be a feature, not a bug, but the more energy a mining rig requires, the more expensive (and expansive) the process becomes. This was an intentional decision made to prevent the blockchain from falling under a single controlling person or group of people. However, the bigger the blockchain network becomes, the worse its impact is on the planet.

Blockchains' current energy consumption rates aren't scalable, but there are some blockchains moving toward environmentally friendly processes. Ethereum has a blockchain called the Beacon Chain that uses PoS and is 99 percent more energy efficient than the main blockchain. It is expected that the Beacon Chain will be merged with the main Ethereum blockchain, and once these two blockchains combine and rely on PoS as a consensus mechanism, Ethereum's blockchain will become 99 percent more energy efficient overall![52] Before other blockchains can expand any further, their energy demands must be reduced.

---

50   "Comparisons." CCAF.io. Accessed June 16, 2022. https://ccaf.io/cbeci/index/comparisons.

51   "Bitcoin Energy Consumption Index." Digiconomist, April 20, 2022. https://digiconomist.net/bitcoin-energy-consumption.

52   Stevens, Robert. "What Is 'The Merge'? Ethereum's Move to Proof of Stake." Decrypt. Decrypt, June 4, 2022. https://decrypt.co/resources/what-merge-ethereum-move-proof-stake.

Government Regulation

Countries are struggling to wrap their heads around blockchain applications, and in many cases, they come up with ideas just in time for more complex advancements in the technology. (Think of the classic onscreen hi-jinks where two characters desperately try to manage products on a conveyor belt—as soon as they get it under control, the belt speeds up and there's even more to manage!) The bigger problem is that the governments are missing the point. As governing bodies struggle to regulate new technology, they accidentally reinforce why the blockchain exists in the first place: to separate society from controlling authorities.

There is a conflict in blockchain technology between regulation and anonymity. Blockchains are supposed to be anonymous. While anonymity is a part of the draw for most people, governments are concerned about what implications that kind of anonymity can have. Scammers can move around in the shadows much easier when everyone operates in digital darkness. Before we see world governments adopt blockchain-based systems in government processes like ID verification, finances, and tax records, they want to be sure the systems are safe from singular shady characters.

Governments know they need blockchain-based regulations, and several governments are already taking steps toward little security victories. The United States is passing regulations for energy impact, self-governing organizations, and tax requirements for digital assets.[53] South Korea formed the Digital Assets Committee to take charge of monitoring the new crypto sector.[54] The European Union (EU) is working on implementing a framework for regulating cryptocurrency, especially

---

[53] Donevan, Connor, and Patrick Jarenwattananon. "There's a New Plan to Regulate Cryptocurrencies. Here's What You Need to Know." NPR. NPR, June 14, 2022. https://www.npr.org/2022/06/14/1104303982/crypto-bitcoin-stablecoin-regulation-senate.

[54] Donevan, Connor, and Patrick Jarenwattananon. "New South Korean Regulatory Chief Promises More 'Fairness' for Crypto Investors." Crypto News, June 1, 2022. https://cryptonews.com/news/new-south-korean-regulatory-chief-promises-more-fairness-for-crypto-investors.htm.

in the wake of Russia's invasion of Ukraine. The EU imposed sanctions on Russia and wants to ensure those sanctions aren't avoided via cryptocurrency's anonymity.[55] These regulatory efforts are likely only the tip of the iceberg. It's fair to expect many more regulations before the blockchain is as fundamental to society as the Internet.

Communication, Communication, Communication

Even if blockchain technology overcomes every other obstacle, it's still almost useless if it exists in a vacuum. Blockchains are great for storing and securing data, but what happens when more than one industry needs to share the same information? If blockchains are meant to make our lives more streamlined, they must be able to streamline cross-blockchain communication. Right now, each blockchain network uses its own language. If two blockchains are to work together, they require a translator to communicate.

For example, if a user wants to invest in Bitcoin and wants to move money to Ether, they need a third-party app to conduct a currency exchange because the two blockchains can't communicate directly. Three projects, Aion, Wanchain, and Polkadot, are working to build a mechanism for transferring data and assets between blockchains directly. With these programs, a user could exchange Bitcoin for Ether without needing a third party application to facilitate the transfer.

With thousands of blockchains running parallel with one another, they will need to communicate in a way that creates smooth interoperability. Interoperability doesn't only apply blockchain-to-blockchain. Consider that other, older systems speak different languages as well. Since it's unrealistic to replace *all* modern data solutions with blockchains overnight, early blockchains also need a way to communicate with legacy infrastructure.

---

[55] "Opening Remarks by Commissioner McGuinness at the ECON Committee Structured Dialogue." ECON Committee: European Commission, June 14, 2022. https://ec.europa.eu/commission/presscorner/detail/en/SPEECH_22_2321.

Blockchains will only be free to operate at their highest potential when they are capable of communicating with all the other technological advancements made in the last few decades. Before establishing the Internet of Things, where blockchain applications all work together, blockchain pioneers will need to create a universal technology translator. One company is already taking the initiative.

Chainlink is a company currently building an ecosystem of **oracles** to facilitate universal communication. These oracles, entities that connect blockchains to external systems, are designed to collect real-world data and distribute it into blockchain networks. This application allows blockchain-based smart contracts to react to real-world events in a way they couldn't before.

For example, if Alice and Bob want to bet on a soccer game, they could each throw 1 ETH into a smart contract on the blockchain and the winner will receive the pot. But who calls the winner? Since the result of the match is considered "off-chain data," the blockchain has no way of knowing the outcome without a user's input...which defeats the purpose, because the user could potentially lie. If Alice and Bob use Chainlink to set up their bet, an oracle can connect to the smart contract, pull the outcome of the game directly from the sports network's website, and supply the results without any user involved. This protects the blockchain *and* the results of the bet.[56]

The Ol' Ball and (Block)chain

Ask a couple married for longer than a decade if their relationship is perfect, and they'll likely laugh at the thought. Ask the same couple if their relationship is successful, and they'll be more likely to take the question seriously. Little victories, continuous growth, and strong foundations give people hope for success in times of change—whether it's a newly wedded lifestyle or a newly disruptive innovation.

---

[56] "What Is an Oracle in Blockchain?" Explained | Chainlink, September 14, 2021. https://chain. link/education/blockchain-oracles.

There is no guarantee that the blockchain will succeed, but it will certainly fail without public support while it improves. Blockchain news throws the public into a frenzy when they're about crypto crashes, carbon footprints, and missed opportunities. Successful blockchain ventures aren't as prominent in the media because the ones with messy endings create better buzz. Who wants to read an article titled "Blockchain Doing Fine" when they could pick up "In The Middle of Summer, Fear Sets in Over Crypto Winter"? And when every other blockchain-based disaster is paired with an equally catchy headline, how will the public ever appreciate the technology?

In reality, the blockchain *is* celebrating little victories every day, but they're happening behind the scenes. New companies are using the blockchain to improve their systems. Blockchain stakeholders are excited about the potential of future applications. Current business applications may not be perfect, but the technology is growing. If blockchain keeps moving in the right direction, it may only be a matter of years before it is finally embraced by the public at large.

Once the public understands the blockchain's potential to grow into a promising innovation, the technology stands a better chance at solving some of our toughest problems. Despite the blockchain's occasional failures, bad days, and hard moments, stick with it. There may come a day when the blockchain shows up and asks *you* to tie the knot.

CHAPTER 10

Engaging with Blockchain

There once was a time when nobody had an email address. The idea of having a digital mailbox that one could access anywhere in the world on the Internet was completely foreign. After all, what was this new Internet thing? What were these new computer labs in hotel lobbies? And how would email and the Internet be better than good old fashioned phone calls on good old fashioned telephone lines? Today, the answers to these questions are so rudimentary that anyone who can't answer them has probably been living under a rock. Yet these are the exact types of questions people are beginning to ask about the blockchain, and without sincere answers many people will resist engaging with the Next Big Thing.

It's time to move beyond the basics of blockchain. The previous chapters covered how the blockchain can solve industry problems like corporate control, parasitic middleman businesses, and a lack of transaction transparency. The blockchain's history shows how it grew to become the Next Big Thing, and how its functions have changed on a technical level. The history also explains how blockchain applications of the past and present will influence future applications both in the business world and on a peer-to-peer level. A deeper understanding of the blockchain reveals some of the current weaknesses blockchain pioneers are working hard to repair.

Now, it's time to explore some of the barriers of entry to the blockchain for lay users, and how to get around them to make this new tech revolutionary. Blockchain barriers can be seen through the same lens early Internet enthusiasts viewed exciting, never-before-seen features that seem commonplace now, like personal accounts, dynamic websites, and file sharing. For simplicity, each of these features will be explored as they apply to the Ethereum blockchain, since that one is the most accessible, user-friendly, and expansive blockchain available at the time of writing.

Finding a Blockchain Wallet

For many of the first-time Internet users, the first step to getting online was setting up an email account. For first-time blockchain users, the first step is setting up an account on the blockchain. Ethereum accounts, for example, are entities that can conduct transactions on Ethereum blockchains. Every Ethereum account has an address, like every Gmail inbox has an email address ending in "@gmail.com." Each user's address (public key) allows them to send and receive ETH from their account. While Google stores all their users' emails and information, Ethereum does not store anything about its users except transaction records. Therefore, users need a separate entity to manage the details inside their Ethereum accounts. That's what blockchain wallets do.

Blockchain wallets are less like the traditional leather, fabric, or duct tape objects we keep in our pockets. They're called "wallets" because they provide users a way to access and manage their funds, but they function more like the inside of our email or online banking accounts. Users can use wallets to view their balance, send transactions, and more. Like email addresses, some users might have more than one wallet—one for their most important data, one for their casual data, and one for the "spam" data. (Yes, I signed up for CryptoKitties, but I don't need to play with my digital cats every day!)

When choosing a wallet, there are several options to consider. Physical blockchain wallets are pieces of hardware that lets users store data offline in the most secure way. This is comparable to a work email address purposed for sending and receiving sensitive information. Mobile wallets are more casual. Users can hook their mobile wallet up to their phone to make data accessible from anywhere. These wallets trade some security for ease of access. There are desktop wallets, which are meant for managing accounts through Mac, Windows, or Linux operating systems. And then there are web wallets, which exist online and can only be accessed through a web browser—a phone, computer, or another smart device.

The type of blockchain wallet best for each user depends on the user's intended use. People looking to casually explore features on the blockchain may opt for a mobile or web wallet. These wallets are easily accessible, user-friendly, and most of them can store multiple types of data such as different cryptocurrencies. However, users hoping to engage in cryptocurrency trading might consider buying a physical wallet to better secure their funds. Mobile, web, and desktop wallets have their own security features, but serious investors may feel more comfortable with a physical asset like a USB drive they can keep on a keychain, or a hard drive they can store in a safe. And the best part is that wallets don't store blockchain data themselves, so they're easily interchangeable. If a user decides on a mobile wallet and wants a physical wallet later, they can switch without issue.

Here are some questions to think about when choosing a wallet for yourself:

Am I new to cryptocurrency?

Am I looking to explore for fun or to trade assets and make serious cash?

Do I want to connect my traditional bank account to my wallet?

Will I want to expand beyond Ethereum and ETH in the future?

Among the wallets popular with beginners, MetaMask leads the pack. MetaMask wallets were some of the first to appear on the Ethereum blockchain, and they remain the most popular today for their easy-to-use interface. MetaMask has a Chrome extension as well as a mobile app. While it doesn't offer some of the more serious features other wallets offer—like fraud alerts or withdrawal limits—MetaMask allows users to buy ETH with a bank card, explore Ethereum dapps, swap tokens for ones on other blockchains, and (if users are feeling lucky) MetaMask allows high volume purchases of cryptocurrency.

Setting up a mobile MetaMask wallet is almost as easy as setting up an email. However, while you create your own email address and password, that is not the case with the blockchain wallet. When you sign up for a wallet, you receive a unique **secret recovery phrase**, also known as a seed phrase. This phrase is an all-access pass to the wallet. It is an alternative to the private keys discussed in previous chapters, and it is encrypted and decrypted behind closed doors. Don't worry, it's just as secure as other types of private keys.

Wallet creation generates a public key as well as a private key, which gives users their "address" on the blockchain. Public keys work like email addresses because users can provide it to access Ethereum's many dapps. Unlike email addresses, though, users aren't creating new accounts every time they sign in to a new dapp. Users' access to everything Ethereum is all linked to the same account on the blockchain, which makes managing access much easier. No more remembering thousands of passwords—it's all inside the wallet!

Buying Cryptocurrency

Blockchain wallets have many functionalities, but they are most commonly used to manage cryptocurrency. Cryptocurrency is the lifeblood flowing through most blockchain applications. In Ethereum's case, users need ETH to participate in most dapps because using the dapps costs transaction fees, which go toward rewarding the blockchain miners behind the scenes.

The methods for buying cryptocurrency depend on the wallets users choose. Many wallets, like MetaMask, work with crypto-payment companies to help perform transactions. These services allow users to make ETH purchases with a credit card, debit card, direct transfer, or even another cryptocurrency.

Transak is one of the more popular options for buying cryptocurrency, especially for MetaMask users. Transak automatically plugs in a suggested amount of traditional currency (like USD) to spend on ETH depending on how the cryptocurrency is performing on the open market. The screen breaks down transactions based on the traditional currency, the total fees associated with the transaction, and the current exchange rate. The total is an estimation of how much ETH users will receive. Below the total, there is a box for **slippage** (Transak's price difference from the market price) and a box for the Average Processing Time. Each estimate is based on how many miners are available, how many transactions are waiting for approval, how quickly the market price is changing, and more.

Before the transaction completes, Transak and most other crypto-payment companies will ask for verification information. Users must provide their name, email, birthday, Social Security number, and a copy of their driver's license or ID card. This might seem counterintuitive to the blockchain's anonymity and transparency features, but it's part of a security process called **Know Your Customer**, or KYC. KYC became a mandatory process for financial institutions as early as the 1990s, but the requirements have expanded alongside technology advancements.[57] Since most crypto-payment companies are still considered financial institutions, they must perform KYC checks on all new customers.

After the KYC process is complete, transactions can be verified and users can purchase cryptocurrency. The transaction will appear inside the wallet in a matter of minutes. Once a record of the transaction is in the wallet, it's also on the blockchain, and users can see which block

---

[57] "Know Your Customer in Banking." Thales Group. Accessed June 17, 2022. https://www. thalesgroup.com/en/markets/digital-identity-and-security/banking-payment/issuance/ id-verification/know-your-customer.

their information is stored in. From the moment it's verified until the end of the world, that transaction will be a small piece of an infinitely growing technology.

Exploring Dapps

Once users set up with their wallet of choice and buy some cryptocurrency to fuel their participation, they are free to explore the future of the blockchain through dapps. Many of the dapps available today are still experimental. And while some haven't caused enough disruption to attract mainstream headlines, others have been successful at using blockchain technology to revolutionize their industries. There are four main categories for dapps on Ethereum: Finance, Art and Collectibles, Gaming, and Technology.[58]

Finance

If users are looking to invest in cryptocurrencies like ETH, then they'd do well to look into financial dapps. Financial dapps focus on building out applications for cryptocurrencies. The most popular tend to be those that give users a way to lend and borrow cryptocurrency.

For example, Aave is a platform run by a DAO that allows users to earn interest on their cryptocurrency the same way banks award small amounts of interest to their customers. Aave users can also borrow cryptocurrency against their collateral across multiple blockchain networks, so if one cryptocurrency stock drops and the other rises, users can adjust their funds accordingly. And since Aave is a DAO, any user who stores cryptocurrency also receives a stake in the company and can vote on new proposals, upgrades, and assets.

---

[58] "Decentralized Applications (Dapps)." ethereum.org. Ethereum. Accessed June 17, 2022. https://ethereum.org/en/dapps.

Financial dapps are best for users looking to make money with ETH or other cryptocurrencies. There are dapps like Uniswap, Matcha, and 1inch that help users swap tokens and set trading restrictions on their wallet to avoid draining it. Other dapps like Polymarket, Augur, and Loopring monitor different markets in the cryptocurrency space and help users see the big picture while they're investing. There are even apps for crowdfunding, like Gitcoin Grants, where users can contribute to community products in exchange for rewards—kind of like Kickstarter, but with more participation and less prank projects.

Art and Collectibles

People more in touch with their creative side who want to share it with the digital world will find plenty of exciting dapps in the Art and Collectibles tab on Ethereum's website. There are dapps for digital artworks (paintings, drawings, and photography), marketplaces for trading digital collectibles, and even platforms for musicians to revolutionize the way they share music with their fanbase. Artists actually have a lot to gain for utilizing these kinds of dapps.

Art and Collectibles dapps focus on digital ownership, specifically as it relates to digital artwork, like NFTs. These dapps help artists earn a higher profit from their original works than traditional art markets because artists' works are linked to them on the blockchain. No matter how many times the artwork changes digital hands, tokenized art proves ownership for all to see. All artwork can be traced back to its original creator, who never worries about their digital signature being covered or removed. Intermediaries that siphon profit from creatives are replaced with dapps.

Art and Collectible dapps give users new, more accessible ways to support artists. While traditional sites like Etsy, Redbubble, and Amazon Handmade provide a platform for artists to sell works, they also take large portions of the artists' profit as payment. This causes the prices of artists' goods to rise so they can still profit after Etsy takes its 25 percent cut. Dapps like Foundation and SuperRare are platforms to invest directly in an artist through their unique artwork. The dapps are decentralized, not middlemen, which means the artists receive all the profit when a user buys from them. And since proof of ownership can always be linked back to the artist, the artist can receive a cut of profit every time their work is bought and sold beyond the initial sale.

While some of the artistic dapps are simple digital marketplaces, some of them offer more interactive options for users. Async Art is a platform that gives users the ability to create a piece of "living art." Users can create artwork (linked to them through their digital signature) and other users can add layers on top. If UserA draws a stick-figure man, UserB can add a layer on top and draw another man, a cat, a hat, or a baseball bat. UserC can add another layer and add a background that makes the whole picture seem like it's underwater or out in space. Each new artist in the community can contribute layers to a master image to create a collaborative, expressive piece of art. Once the work is done, all participating artists can choose to sell or trade their art and share the profits together.

Another more interactive dapp is Audius, a decentralized streaming platform. On Audius, musicians can share music (completed or in-progress), build a fanbase, and monetize their music without signing a record deal and sacrificing creative freedom. Since the platform is on the blockchain, records of their music are immutable and timestamped. The entire Audius community is made of its users, whether they're listeners, artists, or developers. The music player is as easy to use as Spotify or Apple Music, but the musicians receive a *much* larger share of the profit generated by people listening to their works.

In the digital collectibles space, users can trade cards the way their parents, grandparents, and great-grandparents swapped trading cards, but they can do it without meeting down by the soda fountain. In addition to MLB All-Stars or ultra-rare Pokémon, users can swap digital artwork on OpenSea, Rarible, and marble.cards. Users can even trade digital ticket stubs! Proof of Attendance Protocol, or POAP, is a digital marketplace where users collect NFTs to prove they were at a virtual or in-person event. Those NFTs can enter users into raffles, let them vote or collaborate on new POAP projects, or be displayed on a POAP profile for bragging rights.

Gaming

Blockchain-based gaming opens up a whole new world for video game enthusiasts. Whether users enjoy games like Candy Crush, Mario Kart, or Call of Duty, gaming dapps use collectibles with real-world value to provide players across all genres with tangible incentives to play. When a user's avatar picks up a sword from the local blacksmith, that sword has a value that can be translated into cryptocurrency. Winning an online race results in real-world rewards. And all of this value can be reinvested in the game to keep playing, or withdrawn in cash to buy a celebratory drink.

If a player's favorite video games involve building communities and unique worlds, there's a dapp for that. It's called Voxel, and it's a virtual world where players can buy a parcel of land and design it however they want. The game uses single building blocks, which gives it a Minecraft-feel. Players can fill the land with unique creatures and characters, and once the parcel is complete they can sell it, trade it, or post it for other players to visit.

If players are less into worldbuilding and would rather battle creatures and conquer lands, Axie Infinity may be a better fit. Players can fight, breed, and trade creatures called Axies. Players can build up an Axie army to fight bigger enemies and battle against other players in tournaments with real-world rewards. Axie Infinity also gives players a home base that can generate resources for selling or upgrading equipment. The more users play, the more cryptocurrency they earn.

The complexity behind gaming on the blockchain is almost unimaginable—every "transaction" is recorded on the blockchain, which includes data like the number of critical hits in a battle, the size of a loot chest, and the color of a character's hair. Since the transactions are public, no gamers can get away with cheating to win a Battle Royale.

Even the user's save data exists within their Ethereum account so no companies can corrupt, lose, or erase it. As more dapps appear on Ethereum, there will be even more gaming options with even more mind-boggling features.

Technology

This final category is a catch-all for dapps with promising futures and wide applications. Here, developers can upload their tools, join community-based projects for new dapps, and access or rent computer power to others. The technology section is where those looking to join the ever-growing community of blockchain-based businesses can find the tools they need to build on Ethereum's foundation.

A dapp called radicle.xyz provides decentralization for decentralized developers! If a group of like-minded developers want to design a new platform on Ethereum's blockchain, they can use radicle.xyz to collaborate on a P2P network. Imagine collaborating on a document with a group of strangers in Google Docs. All edits are recorded, all parties have an equal stake, and everyone can collaborate in real time. However, since the dapp is blockchain-based, no third party stores their project. There's no risk of losing their progress to a data breach or server failure. Plus, when the project is finished, each member's digital signature prevents one developer from claiming the project as their own.

Since blockchain technology is complex enough to learn about *using*, some dapps exist solely to slow down and teach developers about *building* for blockchains. Education Ecosystem (EE) is a dapp that gives developers a chance to explore new technologies in a practical ecosystem. Experienced blockchain users can develop and upload lessons for newer users to learn from. Then, newer users can practice developing from the safety of the EE ecosystem, a sterile environment that won't blow up a user's entire operating system in the case of a fatal error. Whether it's a tutorial on designing a new video game, a new digital marketplace, or a simple smart contract, new blockchain developers can come to EE for lessons designed by people who were once just like them.

Web 3.0 is based on the blockchain and all of its possibilities for the future. The sooner people choose to get involved with what's going on with this Next Big Thing, the sooner lives will be safer, simpler, and superior. Whether someone is in the market for a driverless minivan or simply looking to make a few coins playing online Solitaire, the best version of the future is blockchain-based.

CONCLUSION

It's easy to feel inferior when learning a brand new subject. The excitement that comes from learning can be quickly crushed when more knowledgeable people step in to correct, refute, and lecture. However, after graduating from novice to expert, it's easy to forget what it was like to be a beginner. This is the Curse of Knowledge, and as excited as I am to keep learning about blockchain technology, this curse plagues most interactions on the subject.

The Curse of Knowledge is a phenomenon that extends far beyond the fields of blockchain. I once had a real estate client, a farmer, who wanted my advice on a new ranch he hoped to buy. I knew nothing about farming, but I agreed to sit in on a meeting with his ranch hands later that week and offer my perspective.

On the day of the meeting I wore a navy blue pantsuit, black business pumps, and carried a white leather laptop purse. I collapsed awkwardly into an empty seat and adjusted the height up four notches. Meanwhile, my client and his four ranch hands piled into the conference room in ripped blue jeans, muddy button-ups, and steel-toed boots. I felt like a spring chicken in a coop full of roosters.

"First up, we've got the County coming next week," a farmer with a thick mustache said, "And we've gotta prove we're using the old barn for agritourism if we wanna keep our zoning benefits."

"What does agritourism mean?" I asked, trying to keep up.

"The old barn is a mess," another farmer grumbled, "Unless showing folks inside and saying' 'Look at this mess!' counts as agritourism, we're not doing it here."

"What is agritourism?" I asked again a little louder. The farmer closest to me, a gruff guy with what I hoped was mud caked in his eyebrow, shot me a sideways look. The rest ignored me and continued.

"It might count," the mustachioed farmer chuckled, "And we need the fields around it, so we gotta come up with a plan."

"What does agritourism mean?" I asked a third time.

Again, no one answered me. *Is it because I'm a woman?* I thought. *Is it the suit? Or is agritourism really that basic of a term for farmers?*

I know now that agritourism (any business activity that brings visitors to a farm or ranch) is such a common term among farmers that I looked dumb for asking about it. The farmers couldn't be bothered to fill in Ms. Pants Suit while discussing business! Unfortunately, I didn't learn anything useful during that meeting because I was too busy wondering if visitors to a farm were called agritourists (they're not).

"Alright then," my client said when their meeting was over. "We've got some real estate decisions to make." He motioned to me, indicating it was my turn to lead the discussion.

Then, although I didn't realize it at the time, I proceeded to do the same thing to those men that they'd done to me. I didn't slow down to explain what preliminary reports, CC&Rs, or contingency options were. And while the men shot each other some confused looks, no one asked me any questions. No one wanted to admit to Ms. Pants Suit that they needed a refresher on what's in an NHD report, so no one learned anything. In a matter of minutes, I found myself on both sides of the Curse of Knowledge.

When the meeting ended, every attendee left the room more confused than before. I was still wondering about agritourism, and the farmers weren't confident in their real estate options. We failed to break down concepts with basic, entry level language, and therefore isolated each other on both ends of the meeting. It was a missed opportunity for us to learn from each other and do business together.

The Curse of Knowledge is so common because when people gain new knowledge they tend to be so eager to use it that they forget other people have yet to learn what they've learned. It's a problem that stunts many people's intrigue and passion for learning. And as beginners learn more about blockchain, if they aren't conscious of this tendency, they'll end up isolating a lot of people who may one day *need* this knowledge.

Blockchain technology isn't going anywhere. It's like a new highway, freshly paved with the finest asphalt and lined with bright new paint. As more people choose to travel along the blockchain, more roadside attractions will pop up along its route—cryptocurrency markets, data storage solutions, and decentralized apps to name a few. The road won't stay pristine for long—potholes will form, lines will fade, fender benders will happen—but like other foundational parts of society, experts will continuously work to improve it.

There will be people who use every bump in the road as an omen for the blockchain's downfall, but only because they don't yet understand its implications. Every time a cryptocurrency crashes, waves of critics clog up online forums with variations on the sentiment, "I told you so." They use the crashes as evidence that the cryptocurrency, and therefore the blockchain, is nothing to be excited about. There are valid reasons to criticize the world of cryptocurrency (that's a story for another book... stay tuned), but cryptocurrency is only one blockchain application among many with the potential to change the world.

The possibilities for blockchain applications are only as limited as our collective imagination. Blockchain is on its way to becoming just as influential as the Internet...and will likely end up *more* influential. After all, not even the Internet could save Americans from the DMV.

Blockchain technology can improve daily life for millions of people. Dapps allow users to better control their personal data and participate more directly with the communities they enjoy. Whether people would rather spend their spare time gaming, making music and works of art, or streaming your favorite shows, dapps help close the gap between people and their favorite pastimes.

The goal of this book is not to teach everything there is to know about the blockchain. It's not about becoming a blockchain expert overnight—it's about providing the tools needed to participate in blockchain-based conversations. It's to bring people along at a basic, easy-to-understand pace. That way, by the time the blockchain transforms the way every average Joe orders a Big Mac, even *he* understands not to share his private key with the Drive-Thru cashier.

Now that you know how efficient the blockchain can make the world, you'll have trouble ignoring how *inefficient* the world is today. At work, you'll notice processes that could be improved with the blockchain. You'll think about it every time you reach for your wallet full of cash, cards, and slips of paper. At home, you'll wish the blockchain could tell you whether the chicken in the back of your fridge is still safe to eat.

No one, not even the blockchain experts, knows everything about this new tech because it's still in its infancy. Blockchain technology is still a ways off from full-on integration with everyday society, but its impact will forever change the course of human history. The blockchain is a disruptive innovation, and although it hasn't transformed much of life yet, its impact has already reached industries from healthcare to horticulture.

The blockchain is definitively *not* a phase, and there's still plenty to learn about how it's going to shape the future.

GLOSSARY

Big Data - Extremely large data sets that may be analyzed computationally to reveal patterns, trends, and associations, especially relating to human behavior and interactions.

Block - A package of data on a blockchain.

Blockchain - A digital ledger made up of a chain of blocks.

Centralized/Centralization - Describes a system or process controlled by one group or within one location.

Consensus - A general agreement among participants.

Consensus Mechanism - A process blockchain validators follow to achieve consensus in a democratic fashion to add a block to a chain.

Consortium Blockchain - A blockchain that allows multiple organizations to collaborate control across a decentralized network.

Content Delivery Network (CDN) - A distributed group of servers which work together to provide fast delivery of Internet content.

Content Management System (CMS) - Computer software used to manage the creation and modification of digital content.

Cryptoasset - A digital asset that uses cryptography to regulate its value and authenticity.

Cryptography - A process that scrambles data for the transmission of secure messages among two or more participants.

Cryptographic Key - A string of numbers that point to an address or wallet in a blockchain.

Decentralized/Decentralization - Describes a system or process distributed amongst its users rather than controlled by one group or within one location.

Decentralized Apps (dapps) - Apps that run on the blockchain without a central authority or location.

Decentralized Autonomous Organization (DAO) - A cooperative collectively owned by its members designed to replace centralized management structures.

DeFi - The abbreviation of "decentralized finance."

Distributed Ledger Technology (DLT) - A decentralized database managed by multiple participants that records information.

Full Node - Nodes that maintain a full copy of the ledger and have the ability to validate, accept, and reject blockchain transactions.

Genesis Block - The first block on a chain that contains initial data for other blocks to build from.

Hard Fork - A change to the software protocol where all previously valid blocks on the blockchain are made invalid (or vice versa.) All nodes and users must upgrade to the new version, so nothing is backwards compatible.

Hash - A fixed-length output returned from a hash algorithm for maintaining consensus on a blockchain.

Hash Function - An algorithm designed to create a fixedlength output regardless of the input's length.

Hybrid Blockchain - A blockchain that combines features from private and public blockchains to meet specific needs.

Immutable - Unchanging over time or unable to be changed.

Internet of Things (IoT) - The digitally connected world that exists between everyday physical devices embedded with Internet connectivity, sensors, and communication hardware.

Know Your Customer (KYC) - A mandatory process of identifying and verifying customer identities when opening a new financial account.

Ledger - A documented collection of data.

Merkle Tree - A data structure divided into layers to relate nodes with a single root associated with them.

Middleman Business - Businesses that operate by acting as an intermediary between two or more parties in a transaction.

Miner - A participant on the blockchain responsible for using a consensus mechanism to validate transactions and add new blocks to a chain.

Multi-Factor Authentication (MFA) - A verification process that uses multiple inputs to verify a user's permission to access an account or accounts.

Node - One of multiple machines that hosts a copy of the blockchain, validates its transactions, and communicates with other machines.

Non-Fungible Tokens (NFTs) - Unique digital assets that contain identifying information recorded in smart contracts.

Nonce - Abbreviation for "number only used once," a number added to the end of a block's hash on the blockchain for added security.

Partial Node - Nodes that do not store complete ledgers, but download the part they require to verify new blocks.

Peer-to-Peer (P2P) - Describes a process that allows two parties to interact without the need for an intermediary or third party.

Private Blockchain - A blockchain managed by a network administrator and requires consent for participants to join the network.

Private Key - An alphanumeric code that allows full access to an account or wallet on the blockchain.

Proof-of-Activity (PoA) - A consensus mechanism that combines PoW and PoS systems; the mining process works the same as PoW, but once a block is successfully validated, the PoS method chooses which miner's block is added to the chain.

Proof-of-Burn (PoB) - A consensus mechanism that requires transactors to send small amounts of their tokens to inaccessible wallets.

Proof-of-Capacity (PoC) - A consensus mechanism that allows nodes on the blockchain network to share memory space with others to mine available cryptocurrency.

Proof-of-Stake (PoS) - A consensus mechanism in which cryptocurrency owners validate block transactions based on the number of coins a validator stakes.

Proof-of-Work (PoW) - A consensus mechanism for verifying transactions with computing power.

Public Blockchain - Open networks that allow anyone to participate in the network.

Public Key - An alphanumeric code that serves as a unique identifier for an account or wallet on the blockchain.

satoshi - The unit of measurement for Bitcoin amounts smaller than one whole Bitcoin.

Secret Recovery Phrase - A string of words assigned to a user that allows access to their blockchain wallet. Also known as a seed phrase.

Slippage - When purchasing cryptocurrency from a third party, the difference between the party's price and the market price is called slippage.

Smart Contract - An agreement between two parties that self-executes when its terms are met and automatically cancels when their terms are not met.

Soft Fork - A change to software protocol where only previously valid transaction blocks are made invalid. Because old nodes will recognize the new blocks as valid, a soft fork is backwards-compatible.

Trustless - Describes a system in which trust in a third party is not required to complete processes or transactions.

Token - A digital representation of ownership stored on the blockchain.

Tokenization - The process of transforming ownership rights for a physical or virtual asset into one or more digital tokens stored and exchanged on a blockchain.

Transaction fees - A fee users pay to use dapps on blockchain networks. Transaction fees are similar to service charges.

Validation - The process a miner follows to ensure transactions added to the blockchain are legitimate.

Wallet - Software or devices that contain public and private keys, allowing users to store cryptocurrency or other digital assets.

NOTES

Introduction: The Curse of Knowledge

Der Naturen Bloeme: The Flower Of Nature (ca. 1350). The Public Domain Review. (n.d.). Retrieved August 29, 2022, from https://public-domainreview.org/collection/ jacob-van-maerlant-der-naturen-bloeme/

2. Webvolution

Bruttig, Spencer. "Here's How the Cold War Helped Create the Internet We Know and Love Today." wusa9.com, December 6, 2019. https://www.wusa9.com/article/news/nation-world/ this-week-in-history-how-the-internet-was-created-during-the-cold-war/.

Techopedia. "What Is the Defense Advanced Research Projects Agency (DARPA)?" Techopedia.com. Techopedia, October 24, 2012. https://www.techopedia.com/ definition/6727/defense-advanced-research-projects-agency-darpa.

Schwartz, John. "Dot-Com Is Dot-Gone, and the Dream With It." The New York Times. The New York Times, November 25, 2001. https://www.nytimes.com/2001/11/25/style/ dot-com-is-dot-gone-and-the-dream-with-it.html.

McCullough, Brian. "A Revealing Look at the Dot-Com Bubble of 2000 - And How It Shapes Our Lives Today." ideas.ted.com, December 4, 2018. https://ideas.ted.com/ an-eye-opening-look-at-the-dot-com-bubble-of-2000-and-how-it-shapes-our-lives-today/.

Verma, Pragati. "Evolution of Web." DEV Community. DEV Community, June 21, 2021. https://dev.to/pragativerma18/evolution-of-web-42eh.

3. The Problems Blockchain Solves

Keegan, John, and Alfred Ng. "Life360 Is Selling Precise Location Data on Its Tens of Millions of Users." The Markup, December 6, 2021. https://themarkup.org/privacy/2021/12/06/the-popular-family- safety-app-life360-is-selling-precise-location-data-on-its-tens-of millions-of-user.

Dihuni. "Every Day Big Data Statistics – 2.5 Quintillion Bytes of Data Created Daily." Dihuni.com: Digital Transformation Simplified, April 10, 2020. https://www.dihuni.com/2020/04/10/every-day-big-data-statistics-2-5-quintillion-bytes-of-data-created-daily/.

Tallent, Amanda. "What Personal Data Do Navigation Apps Collect?" MarkTechPost, July 12, 2019. https://www.marktechpost.com/2019/07/12/what-personal-data-do-navigation-apps-collect/.

Fruhlinger, Josh. "Equifax Data Breach FAQ: What Happened, Who Was Affected, What Was the Impact?" CSO Online. CSO, February 12, 2020. https://www.csoonline.com/article/3444488/equifax-data-breach-faq-what-happened-who-was-affected-what-was-the-impact.html.

Sung, Morgan. "It Turns Out Purposely Messing With Your Targeted Ads Isn't a Good Idea." Mashable. Mashable, April 26, 2019. https://mashable.com/article/purposely-engaging-with-weird-ads-isnt-good.

4. The Basics of Blockchain

Frankenfield, Jake. "Distributed Ledger Technology." Investopedia. Investopedia, February 8, 2022. https://www.investopedia.com/terms/d/distributed-ledger-technology-dlt.asp.

Waldman, Jonathan. Blockchain - Blockchain Fundamentals. Microsoft Docs, March 2018. https://docs.microsoft.com/en-us/archive/msdn-magazine/2018/march/blockchain-blockchain-fundamentals.

Cryptopedia Staff. "Trustless Blockchains and Non-Custodial Wallets." Cryptopedia. Cryptopedia, August 11, 2021. https://www.gemini.com/cryptopedia/trustless-meaning-blockchain-non-custodial-smart-contracts.

Nakamoto, Satoshi. "Bitcoin: A Peer-to-Peer Electronic Cash System." Bitcoin.org, October 31, 2008. https://bitcoin.org/bitcoin.pdf.

Hamilton, A. "The Beginning of NFTs - A Brief History of NFT Art." Zeno Fine Art. Zeno Fine Art, March 3, 2022. https://www.zenofin eart.com/blogs/news/the-beginning-of-nfts-a-brief-history-of-nft-art.

Melanie Kramer, Stephen Graves. "Beginner's Guide to NFTs: WhatAre Non-Fungible Tokens?" Decrypt. Decrypt, January 18, 2022. https://decrypt.co/resources/non-fungible-tokens-nfts-explained-guide-learn-blockchain.

Bybit Learn. "Blockchain 3.0." Bybit Learn. Bybit, May 13, 2022. https://learn.bybit.com/glossary/definition-blockchain-3.0/.

5. How Does the Blockchain Work?

Parizo, Christine. "What Are the 4 Different Types of Blockchain Technology?" SearchCIO. TechTarget, May 28, 2021. https://www.techtarget.com/searchcio/feature/What-are-the-4-different-types-of-blockchain-technology.

Tardi, Carla. "Genesis Block Definition." Investopedia. Investopedia, September 8, 2021. https://www.investopedia.com/terms/g/genesis-block.asp.

"Blockchain Explained." Blockchain Explained | Euromoney Learn ing. Accessed June 2, 2022. https://www.euromoney.com/learning/blockchain-explained.

Hayes, Adam. "Proof of Capacity (Cryptocurrency)." Investopedia. Investopedia, February 8, 2022. https://www.investopedia.com/terms/p/proof-capacity-cryptocurrency.asp.

"Steem Bluepaper." Steem. Steemit, Inc., 2017. https://steem.com/steem-whitepaper.
pdf.

6. The Business of Blockchain

Center for Food Safety and Applied Nutrition. "Outbreak of E. Coli O157:H7 Infections
Linked to Chopped Romaine Lettuce Grown in Yuma Region." U.S. Food and Drug
Administration. FDA. Accessed June 7, 2022. https://www.fda.gov/food/outbreaks-
foodborne-illness/fda-investigated-multistate-outbreak-e-coli-o157h7-infections-
linked-romaine-lettuce-yuma-growing.

Tyko, Kelly. "Walmart Recall: Tanimura & Antle Romaine Lettuce Recalled from
More Than 1,000 Walmart Stores Over E. Coli Risk." USA Today. Gannett Satellite
Information Network, November 10, 2020. https://www.usatoday.com/story/money/
shopping/2020/11/10/walmart-recall-2020-romaine-lettuce-tanimura-antle-ecoli-
contamination/6233817002/.

"Blockchain for Financial Services." IBM. Accessed June 7, 2022. https://www.ibm.com/
blockchain/industries/financial-services.

Mulders, Michiel. "Which Major Banks Have Adopted or Are Adopting the Blockchain?"
Blockchain Works. Blockchain Works, June 7, 2022. https://blockchain.works-hub.com/
learn/Which-Major-Banks-Have-Adopted-or-Are-Adopting-the- Blockchain-.

Board of Governors of the Federal Reserve System. "Joint Statement on Crypto-Asset
Policy Sprint Initiative and Next Steps." FDIC, November 23, 2021. https://www.fdic.
gov/news/press-releases/2021/.

CB Insights. "How Blockchain Could Disrupt Banking." CB Insights
Research. CB Insights, July 1, 2021. https://www.cbinsights.com/research/
blockchain-disrupting-banking/.

"The Cost of Food Spoilage: Cargo Data Corp." Cargo Data, June 13, 2018. https://
cargodatacorp.com/cost-food-spoilage/.

"Digital Health Passport." Aetsoft. Accessed July 11, 2022. https://aetsoft.net/products/
digital-health-passport/.

Heller, Nathan. "Estonia, the Digital Republic." The New Yorker, December 11, 2017. https://www.newyorker.com/maga zine/2017/12/18/estonia-the-digital-republic.

Napoli, Robert. "Council Post: How Blockchain Could Revolutionize Cybersecurity." Forbes. Forbes Magazine, March 7, 2022. https://www.forbes.com/sites/ forbestechcouncil/2022/03/04/how-blockchain-could-revolutionize-cybersecurity/.

Daley, Sam. "Wallets, Hospitals and the Chinese Military: 18 Examples of Blockchain Cybersecurity at Work." Built In, April 15, 2022. https://builtin.com/blockchain/ blockchain-cybersecurity-uses.

7. Blockchain in Everyday Life

"Chikn." chikn. Accessed June 9, 2022. https://chikn.farm/.

"Everything You Need to Know about Tokenization." 101 Blockchains, May 5, 2022. https://101blockchains.com/tokenization-blockchain/.

"KTDI Frequently Asked Questions." Known Traveler Digital Identity. World Economic Forum. Accessed June 9, 2022. https://ktdi.org/.

"Blockchain Technology for Digital Contracting." Accenture. Accessed June 9, 2022. https://www.accenture.com/us-en/case-studies/about/ blockchain-contracts-harnessing-new-technology.

CoreLedger. "How Blockchain Makes a Smart Lock Even Smarter." Medium. CoreLedger, September 25, 2019. https://medium.com/coreledger/ how-blockchain-makes-a-smart-lock-even-smarter-520d01176f4b.

Lu, Marcus, ed. "Blockchain Applications: Tokenization of Real Assets." Visual Capitalist, January 25, 2022. https://www.visualcapitalist.com/ blockchain-applications-tokenization-of-real-assets/.

Thomas, Mike. "30 Internet of Things Examples You Should Know." BuiltIn, June 6, 2022. https://builtin.com/internet-things/iot-examples.

Hruska, Joel. "The Internet of Things Has Officially Hit Peak Stupid." ExtremeTech, January 5, 2017. https://www.extremetech.com/electronics/242169-internet-things-officially-hit-peak-stupid-courtesy-smart toaster-griffin-technology.

"Wireless Home Security Alarm System: Simplisafe Features." Wireless Home Security Alarm System | SimpliSafe Features. Accessed June 9, 2022. https://simplisafe.com/meet-the-system.

Thomas, Mike. "9 Companies Helping Create the IoT Smart City." Built In. Accessed June 9, 2022. https://builtin.com/internet-things/iot-smart-city-applications.

8. Blockchain Security

Cryptopedia Staff. "The Dao: What Was the DAO Hack?" Gemini. Cryptopedia, March 16, 2022. https://www.gemini.com/cryptopedia/the-dao-hack-makerdao.

Frankenfield, Jake. "Hard Fork (Blockchain) Definition." Investopedia. Investopedia, May 25, 2022. https://www.investopedia.com/terms/h/hard-fork.asp.

"What Is Blockchain Security?" IBM. Accessed June 14, 2022. https://www.ibm.com/topics/blockchain-security.

Anna Foley, Alex Goldman, and Emmanual Dzotsi, hosts, "The Rainbow Chain." Reply All (podcast), April 7, 2022, accessed June 14, 2022, https://gimletmedia.com/shows/reply-all/j4he7a7/185-the-rainbow-chain

Binance Academy. "Sybil Attacks Explained." Binance Academy. Binance Academy, October 4, 2021. https://academy.binance.com/cs/articles/sybil-attacks-explained.

Falkon, Samuel. "The Story of the DAO - Its History and Consequences." Medium. The Startup, August 12, 2018. https://medium.com/swlh/the-story-of-the-dao-its-history-and-consequences-71e6a8a551ee.

9. Blockchain's Biggest Challenge

Rothberg, Ethan. "Bitcoin's Crashing - Here's Why Warren Buffett Has Hated It All Along." Yahoo! Finance. Yahoo!, June 14, 2022. https://finance.yahoo.com/news/bitcoins-crashing-heres-why-warren-220000034.html.

O'Connell, Justin. "The Future of IOT: Blockchain Biometrics with HYPR." Bitcoinist.com, August 2, 2016. https://bitcoinist.com/future-iot-blockchain-hypr/.

Albert Vein Institute. (2019, October 22). Do you know how amazing your veins are? Albert Vein Institute. Retrieved June 19, 2022, from https://www.albertvein.com/blog/2018/june/do-you-know-how-amazing-your-veins-are-/#:~:text=How%20Fast%20is%20Blood%20Pumped%20Through%20Your%20Body%3F,gallons%20of%20blood%20an%

"Comparisons." CCAF.io. Accessed June 16, 2022. https://ccaf.io/cbeci/index/comparisons.

"Bitcoin Energy Consumption Index." Digiconomist, April 20, 2022. https://digiconomist.net/bitcoin-energy-consumption.

Stevens, Robert. "What Is 'The Merge'? Ethereum's Move to Proof of Stake." Decrypt. Decrypt, June 4, 2022. https://decrypt.co/resources/what-merge-ethereum-move-proof-stake.

Donevan, Connor, and Patrick Jarenwattananon. "There's a New Plan to Regulate Cryptocurrencies. Here's What You Need to Know." NPR. NPR, June 14, 2022. https://www.npr.org/2022/06/14/1104303982/crypto-bitcoin-stablecoin-regulation-senate.

Donevan, Connor, and Patrick Jarenwattananon. "New South Korean Regulatory Chief Promises More 'Fairness' for Crypto Investors." Crypto News, June 1, 2022. https://cryptonews.com/news/new-south-korean-regulatory-chief-promises-more-fairness-for-crypto-investors.htm.

"Opening Remarks by Commissioner McGuinness at the ECON Committee Structured Dialogue." ECON Committee: European Commission, June 14, 2022. https://ec.europa.eu/commission/presscorner/detail/en/SPEECH_22_2321.

"What Is an Oracle in Blockchain?" Explained | Chainlink, September 14, 2021. https://chain.link/education/blockchain-oracles.

10. Engaging with Blockchain

"Know Your Customer in Banking." Thales Group. Accessed June 17, 2022. https://www.thalesgroup.com/en/markets/digital-identity-and-security/banking-payment/issuance/id-verification/know-your-customer.

"Decentralized Applications (Dapps)." ethereum.org. Ethereum. Accessed June 17, 2022. https://ethereum.org/en/dapps.

ACKNOWLEDGMENTS

It took a village to get this project from start to finish. We would like to thank everyone that participated in the process in one way or another. We were inspired by so many. Special thanks to: Jean Griffin, Kevin Griffin, Sonny Alger, Janice Alger, Cheryl Bianco Pirrotta-Alger, Rose Williams, and Ronald Alger.

Leave a Review!

If you enjoyed the book, please help others find it by leaving a review. I would be incredibly thankful.

Customer Reviews

★★★★★ 15

5.0 out of 5 stars ▾

5 star		100%
4 star		0%
3 star		0%
2 star		0%
1 star		0%

Share your thoughts with other customers

Write a customer review

How to leave a review:

- Go to the product detail page for the item. If you've placed an order for the item, you can also go to Your Orders
- Click Write a customer review in the Customer Reviews section.
- Select a Star Rating.
- A green check mark shows for successfully submitted ratings.
- (Optional) Add text, photos, or videos and click Submit.

If you enjoyed the book, visit the blog!

www.KeepUpPublications.com

Sign up and Join the FUN as we create an awesome community!

In return, get some cool stuff like exclusive articles, follow the book adventure, and give your advice on chapters – plus a few surprises!

See you there

Keep Up Publication

Want to understand what blockchain is without all the jargon?

You've come to the right place

Keep Up Publications is a project that is helping people understand how everything we do in the world will change due to the blockchain technology.

When the internet was introduced into the mainstream in the 1990's, no one could have imagined just how much it would change the world. We think blockchain technologies will be even bigger!

Started by a lifelong learner with a diverse background in life experience, education, and interests...Keep Up Publications is a team dedicated to empowering the individual to understand the blockchain from a beginners perspective.

Our blog is where, as an online community, we are mastering blockchain basics for the beginner using a step-by-step process presented in layman terms. Join us as we discover the power of the blockchain and we explore how organizations and industries are reinventing themselves using this new and exciting blockchains technology.

Follow us on our journey as we publish our first book. Blockchain Basics Introduction Handbook: A Practical Non-technical Guide for the Blockchain Beginner is written in an entertaining way using stories, humor, and examples that everyone can relate to.

Most importantly the book breaks down all the technical complex jargon!

Thanks for stopping by and we look forward to sharing this amazing journey with you!

Cheers,
Keep Up Publications Team
www.KeepUpPublication.com

Audiobook available too!

go to Audible.com
and search
by title or author

BLOCKCHAIN
BASICS
INTRODUCTION
HANDBOOK

A Practical Non-technical Guide
for the Blockchain Beginner

MICHELLE SIMMS
KEEP UP PUBLICATIONS

Made in the USA
Middletown, DE
03 February 2023